Transportation

Other Publications:
THE NEW FACE OF WAR
HOW THINGS WORK
WINGS OF WAR
CREATIVE EVERYDAY COOKING
COLLECTOR'S LIBRARY OF THE UNKNOWN
CLASSICS OF WORLD WAR II
TIME-LIFE LIBRARY OF CURIOUS AND UNUSUAL FACTS
AMERICAN COUNTRY
VOYAGE THROUGH THE UNIVERSE
THE THIRD REICH
THE TIME-LIFE GARDENER'S GUIDE
MYSTERIES OF THE UNKNOWN
TIME FRAME
FIX IT YOURSELF
FITNESS, HEALTH & NUTRITION
SUCCESSFUL PARENTING
HEALTHY HOME COOKING
LIBRARY OF NATIONS
THE ENCHANTED WORLD
THE KODAK LIBRARY OF CREATIVE PHOTOGRAPHY
GREAT MEALS IN MINUTES
THE CIVIL WAR
PLANET EARTH
COLLECTOR'S LIBRARY OF THE CIVIL WAR
THE EPIC OF FLIGHT
THE GOOD COOK
WORLD WAR II
HOME REPAIR AND IMPROVEMENT
THE OLD WEST

This volume is one of a series that examines
various aspects of computer technology
and the role computers play in modern life.

UNDERSTANDING COMPUTERS

Transportation

BY THE EDITORS OF TIME-LIFE BOOKS
TIME-LIFE BOOKS, ALEXANDRIA, VIRGINIA

Contents

The Road to Computerization

Without warning, a thunderstorm's wind and rain lash at a car proceeding along a narrow road. Peering through the deluge as he rounds a curve, the driver suddenly sees another automobile pulling out of a driveway just ahead. He slams his foot against the brake pedal, half-expecting to skid out of control on the slick road. Instead, the car comes to a rapid, straight, and safe stop.

Credit for the automobile's perfect performance belongs not to the driver, or even to luck, but to a computer linked to a quartet of electronic sensors tucked near the wheels. Each sensor performs a one-dimensional role: It monitors the velocity of a wheel and sends this information digitally—as a series of electronic pulses—to the computer. In a flash, the computer analyzes the data from the four sensors, judges whether any of the wheels is about to stop turning, and then signals the braking system to briefly relax its efforts to stop the car.

In effect, the computer does what every driver is taught to do under similar conditions: pump the brakes to avert a skid. But unlike the driver, the computer can be depended upon to do it perfectly every time—up to ten times a second.

This antilock braking system is just one of dozens of computer applications giving the automobile remarkable new capabilities—and indeed revolutionizing the entire world of transportation. In recent years, computers have been used to ease the burden on humans in many venues where a task involves a large volume of information or tedious calculations—and especially where error could be catastrophic. Thus it is no surprise that computers aboard ships have virtually taken over navigation, or that computers now operate urban transit systems, track flights for air-traffic controllers, follow the progress of goods shipped across the ocean, and locate empty boxcars for railroad customers.

In the form of microprocessors, computers have proliferated into virtually every nook and cranny of today's cars, planes, and ships. These tiny integrated circuits, which contain thousands of electronic components capable of making intricate calculations, are cheap enough to be given a single specialized job and rugged enough to function reliably through years of exposure to heat, dirt, and moisture. Teamed with sensors that measure physical phenomena such as the rotation of a shaft or the temperature of a gas, microprocessors perform roles ranging from the control of combustion in an automobile's engine to the management of a sixty-ton jet airliner as it comes in for a landing at 150 miles per hour.

SPINOFFS FROM SPACE

Computer technology began to enter the world of transportation in the late 1960s, in part because of a retrenchment at that time in the computer-intensive fields of military and aerospace technology. After landing men on the moon, the United States had begun to slow its space program, and the armed forces were spending money on a war in Southeast Asia, some of which might otherwise have funded research and development efforts.

The recession in the aerospace industry was felt acutely at General Motors' AC Electronics Division in Milwaukee, which had developed guidance and navigation systems for the military and for the Apollo space program. Seeking ways to hold onto valued engineers, the president of General Motors, Edward Cole, brought a group of them into the automobile business. Among the imports was Oliver McCarter, who would eventually become leader of GM's Advanced Engineering Staff. "Ed Cole was an explorer," McCarter later recalled. "He was always trying to do something different." In this instance, "different" meant investigating ways in which computers might be used in the cars that General Motors sold by the millions each year.

There was, at the time, no compelling reason to computerize the family car, as seems evident from the kinds of inventions the former AC engineers came up with. "We had a car," McCarter remembered, "that would monitor the driver's cardiac performance as he drove." Tiny sensors in the steering wheel read pulse rate and strength through the grip of the driver's hands. The aerospace group also developed an automobile radar system that detected obstacles and warned of impending collision.

"These were all very interesting," McCarter said, "but they all had a common problem—money. They were entirely too expensive to put in a car." Even if the cost obstacle could have been overcome, the electronics of the time were far too fragile for automotive service and drew more power than the standard automobile electrical system could furnish.

DIGITALLY UNDOING POLLUTION

Before long, however, the aerospace engineers turned their attention to more practical pursuits. Other automotive engineers were struggling to solve a problem that, to a considerable extent, could be attributed to the very success of the automobile—air pollution. Gasoline-fueled engines had been recognized as a major source of pollutants since the early 1950s, but a decade later, car builders had not moved to correct or even to alleviate the problem. When they eventually did so, in the mid-1960s, it was in grudging response to pollution-control laws that were enacted first by California and later by the federal government.

Gasoline engines harness the energy released when a mixture of gasoline and air is ignited. Under ideal combustion conditions, the only waste products of this interaction are water vapor and carbon dioxide, both relatively harmless gases. But conditions in a car engine are rarely perfect, and as a result, automobile exhaust is foul with pollutants.

The combustion flaws occur in two principal ways. If the fuel-air mixture is excessively rich—too much fuel for the amount of air entering the engine—all the gasoline does not burn, leaving a residue of hydrocarbons (unburned gasoline vapor) and also producing the poison gas carbon monoxide. And if the mixture is too lean—that is, not enough fuel—the engine runs too hot. The high temperature causes nitrogen and oxygen in the air to combine as oxides of nitrogen that, when combined with hydrocarbons in the car's exhaust system, create smog. Driving conditions further complicate things. The desired degree of richness or leanness depends on how much power is needed at any given moment. A mixture too rich for cruising down a highway might be perfect for overtaking and passing another car on a two-lane road.

To some extent, automotive engines were able to control pollutants by mechanical means. First, the mixture was made lean to reduce hydrocarbon formation. Then, to cool the engine slightly and limit the production of oxides of nitrogen, a small amount of exhaust gas was returned to the combustion chamber. Engineers also limited hydrocarbons by pumping a small amount of air into the exhaust manifold; there, the oxygen in the air combined with the unwanted fumes and burned them up.

Implementing this regimen exacted a substantial penalty in performance, however. "In fact," asserted the 1974 edition of *Chilton's Guide to Emission Controls,* a respected primer for auto repairmen, "if you drive a late-model car that does not surge or hesitate at any speed, then someone has probably doctored the car to make it run better."

To eliminate surge and hesitation, the catalytic converter was invented. Spliced into the exhaust pipe, the converter is a canister-like chamber containing pellets of metals such as rhodium, platinum, and palladium. As exhaust gases flow through a catalytic converter, they come in contact with the pellets, which

convert the hydrocarbons, carbon monoxide, and oxides of nitrogen into less harmful gases such as carbon dioxide and water.

The air-fuel mixture could now be made richer so that the engine, by burning more gasoline, would run smoothly and predictably. More pollutants would be produced, but the converter would render them benign, at least in theory. In practice, the effectiveness of this device also depended on conditions inside the engine. Wide swings to either side of "perfect" combustion tended to overload the converter with too many pollutants or too much heat, reducing both its efficiency and its life.

Early on, automotive engineers realized that the ideal solution would be to adjust the air-fuel mixture second-by-second to match driving conditions. They also knew that electronically controlled devices could respond rapidly and accurately enough to do the job. But there was no rush to use them—in part because computers were costly.

The economics of the situation was redefined, however, by a chain of events that began in 1973. That year, an oil embargo by Arab nations caused a sharp rise in the price of gasoline, and shortly thereafter, new government regulations dictated that fuel economy and pollution control would become equally important—to the detriment of smooth engine performance. Computers had not suddenly become cheaper, but now they were indispensable, if the the government's requirements were to be satisfied.

SNIFFING THE EXHAUST
First, engineers mated electronic sensors with catalytic converters to continually measure the oxygen content of the engine's exhaust. High levels of oxygen indicated an air-gasoline mixture that was too lean; low levels were evidence of a mixture that was too rich. The computer quickly analyzed the data, calculated the proper fuel-air mix, and sent signals to the carburetor, where air and gasoline are combined, to either enrich the mixture or make it leaner as required at the moment.

Fuel-injection systems, in which multiple nozzles spray a mist of gasoline into the air as it rushes into a combustion chamber so that each cylinder receives the identical fuel mixture, began to replace the carburetor, a device that often gives cylinders near it a richer mixture than necessary in order to provide distant cylinders with a mixture that is not too lean. Soon computer control was applied to the engine's ignition-timing system to calculate more precisely than ever before when to ignite the fuel mixture in order to maximize fuel economy and minimize pollution. A computer became responsible for setting the car's idle speed, adjusting it to suit weather conditions and the load placed on the engine by accessories such as the air conditioner (pages 28-31).

As sensors and microcomputers proliferated within the car's control systems, the next step became apparent: integration of these separate systems. A centralized, multipurpose computer linked the small, single-minded systems and took up the task of overseeing all of the control operations.

The computerization of the automobile did not end with the engine. Designers and engineers began to ask where else computers might help. Among the other targets, in addition to brakes, have been the car's steering and suspension, heating and air-conditioning systems, the automobile's ability to report on its own ailments, and even a way to have a car seat reset itself to the occupant's favorite position *(pages 32-41)*.

The importance of computers to the automobile world can be seen in their increasing contribution to the cost of a new car. In 1975, the average car contained $60 worth of electronics; in 1985, the value had risen to $585. By 1995, the contribution of computers to the cost of the average car is expected to reach $1,400.

Part of that $1,400 may contribute to the solution of a problem that the proliferation of automotive electronic devices has helped to exacerbate: the complexity of a car's wiring. Computers and the sensors connected to them, as well as the growing array of lights, remote-control door locks, burglar alarms, warning buzzers, and stereo sound systems that embellish many automobiles, have created an electrical nightmare—an unwieldy maze of wires to connect each component to the car's battery. For example, a headlight mounted just six inches from the battery requires that a wire must run from the battery to a switch on the dashboard, and thence to the light. As many as fifty-two wires lead to the car door alone. The result is a wiring harness—the bundle of wires leading from the battery to every electric device—that has become costly to build and, because it is stiff and unwieldy, difficult to install.

Auto engineers are working on ways to greatly simplify the wiring harness. In one approach, called "smart power," most of the switches on the car—the headlight or windshield-wiper switches, for example—are replaced by controllers, devices that emit one or more combinations of ones and zeros when pressed, turned, flipped, or pulled. All of these digital signals, each unlike those produced by any other controller, travel to a central computer over a wire called a communications bus. The computer stores the signal in memory and issues an instruction, also composed of ones and zeros, for electricity to be routed to the component being controlled.

This instruction travels along the communications bus, which also connects the computer to integrated circuits called smart-power chips mounted on many electrical devices in the car. Each of these integrated circuits is a kind of switch, programmed to notice only a few of the many signals transmitted by the computer. Upon receiving a message to turn on the headlights, for instance, the chip closes the circuit between the bulb and a wire carrying electricity from the battery. A different combination of ones and zeros turns the lights off.

In theory, a single power wire could serve the full array of electrical devices built into an automobile. In practice, however, several such circuits are routed around the car. Multiple circuits, each of which contains a fuse

Recording a Flight's Vital Statistics

Since the 1960s, regulations have required commercial aircraft to carry two crashproof recorders, popularly known as black boxes. One is a simple audio recorder that captures the crew's voices. The other is a more complex data-collection device designed to chronicle various features of the plane's performance. Early versions of this flight-data recorder were relatively clumsy affairs that stored information as analog, or continuously varying, traces etched on a spool of foil. Because the recorders could track only four aspects, or parameters, of flight—altitude, speed, heading, and vertical acceleration—they often were little help to investigators when they

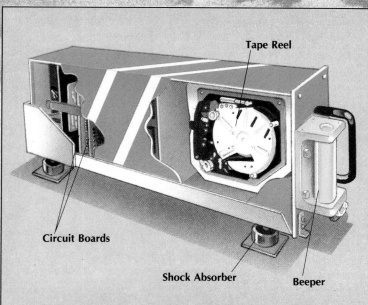

Tape Reel

Circuit Boards

Shock Absorber

Beeper

A Safe Place for Data

A plane's digital recorder stores up to twenty-five hours of flight data on a single reel of magnetic tape; a bank of circuit boards prepares the input from the flight-data acquisition unit *(opposite)* for recording on the tape's six tracks. Encased in a titanium box mounted on four shock absorbers, the recorder is designed to withstand the impact of virtually any crash; special insulation protects against heat and flames. A bright orange casing and two white reflective strips make the unit easier to spot amid wreckage. If the recorder is submerged, a beeper bolted to one end comes to life automatically, attracting the attention of searchers.

were trying to determine the precise cause of an accident.

But computer technology and the advent of microprocessors revolutionized the gathering of flight data. Today's flight-data acquisition unit *(below)* collects, organizes and digitizes analog signals from a host of sensors, permitting the flight recorder to register on magnetic tape dozens of flight parameters, from the plane's attitude—its pitch up and down or roll from side to side—to the status of its many mechanical and electrical systems. If trouble strikes, this wealth of digital data can be used in computer models *(pages 14-15)* to provide a detailed reconstruction of the events that led to calamity.

Capturing flight data. Sensors placed at key locations *(red dots)* throughout an airliner send a steady stream of electrical signals to the flight-data acquisition unit *(white box)*. Direct connections to cockpit instruments provide such information as altitude, heading, pitch, and roll; a sensor in the plane's nose reports on airspeed. Detectors in the wings and tail section indicate the positions of control surfaces, such as the flaps and rudder, while sensors in each engine measure thrust.

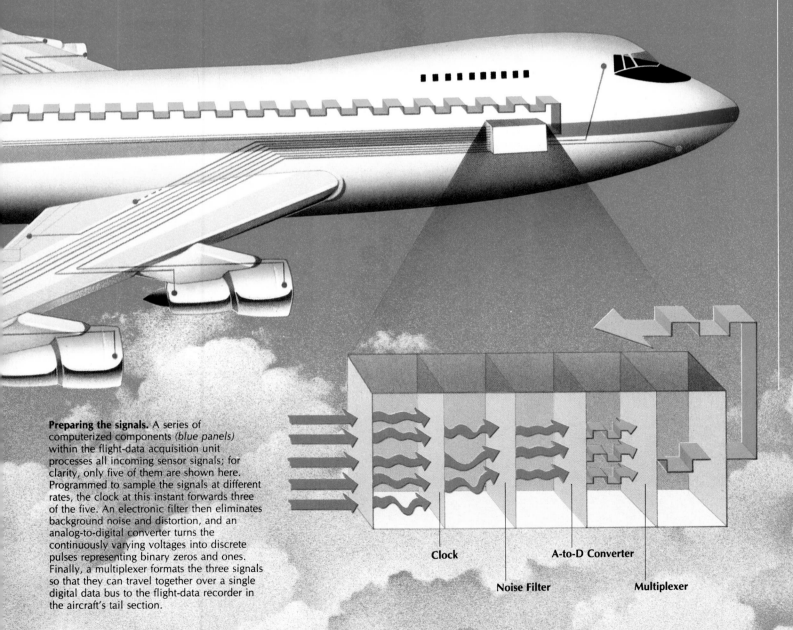

Preparing the signals. A series of computerized components *(blue panels)* within the flight-data acquisition unit processes all incoming sensor signals; for clarity, only five of them are shown here. Programmed to sample the signals at different rates, the clock at this instant forwards three of the five. An electronic filter then eliminates background noise and distortion, and an analog-to-digital converter turns the continuously varying voltages into discrete pulses representing binary zeros and ones. Finally, a multiplexer formats the three signals so that they can travel together over a single digital data bus to the flight-data recorder in the aircraft's tail section.

Clock

Noise Filter

A-to-D Converter

Multiplexer

Tracing the fall. The six computer images below are part of a sequence that allowed investigators to replay Flight 006's plunge. Graphics software produced the outlined image of the plane; flight-recorder data, including pitch, roll, and heading, was used to manipulate the image. Other significant parameters are listed at the top of each display. The control-wheel position, in the center, is represented both numerically and by a needle indicator; negative numbers denote how far to the left the wheel has been turned, and positive numbers how far to the right. The pilot's attempts to raise the nose, by pulling back on the control wheel, were reported separately. Time is shown to tenths of a second directly below the control-wheel needle. A small chart in the upper right corner indicates with vertical lines the amount of thrust from each engine.

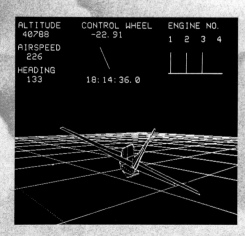

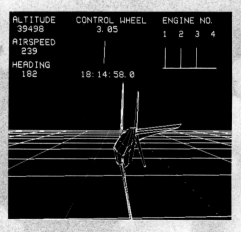

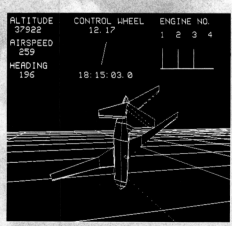

Having lost power in engine four, the plane dips to the right. The autopilot, restricted by its design, cannot turn the control wheel far enough to the left to keep the plane level.

The pilot has assumed manual control, but not soon enough; after twenty-two seconds the tilt has reached almost ninety degrees, and the plane has begun to enter a dive.

Five seconds later, the airspeed has increased by twenty knots and the plane has dropped more than 1,500 feet.

A Graphic Reconstruction

On February 19, 1985, China Airlines Flight 006 was cruising on autopilot at 41,000 feet en route to Los Angeles when, without warning, the Boeing 747 began to fall from the sky. The plane corkscrewed wildly as it plummeted, causing numerous minor injuries among the passengers. Before the pilot regained control, two terrifying minutes had passed and the airliner had dropped more than six miles.

What had gone wrong? To unravel the mystery, analysts turned to the plane's flight recorder. And to help make sense of its stream of numbers, they employed a computer that was programmed to translate selected flight data into a graphic animation of the event. The resulting images made it easier to study, among other things, the responses of the pilot to the developing crisis.

Thrust measurements left no doubt that loss of power in the outer engine on the right wing had started the trouble. A 747 can operate on only three engines, but not while flying on autopilot. The computer simulation helped investigators determine that the pilot, by not disengaging the autopilot right away, had let the situation get out of hand. If, at the first sign of engine failure, he had taken over the controls himself, the near-catastrophe might never have happened.

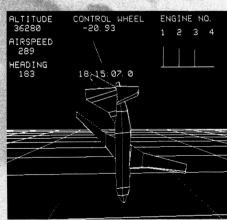
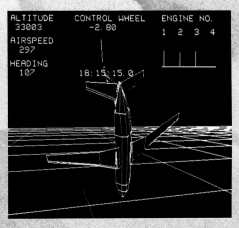
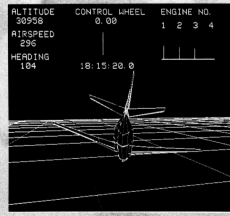

After thirty-one seconds, with the plane pointed almost straight down, the pilot tries to regain control by turning the control wheel to the left, but with no effect.

Still spinning and twisting, the plane continues to plunge headlong. Hopelessly disoriented, the pilot cannot right the craft.

Although the plane appears to be pulling out of its dive in this frame, it will fall another 20,000 feet before the pilot can level off, just in time to avert disaster.

to protect against electrical overloads, prevent the automobile from being totally disabled by a single electrical fault. Furthermore, devices such as the starter motor, which draw immense amounts of current, need thicker power wires than dashboard lights, which draw little current. Providing several power circuits enables engineers to tailor the car's wiring to the components it must serve.

Automobile manufacturers estimate that the simplification of the wiring harness alone justifies designing digital controllers into motorized vehicles. But smart power can do more than streamline the electrical system. It can also aid in troubleshooting repairs. For example, after receiving a signal to "turn on high beams," a headlight chip can be programmed so that it transmits a message over the communications bus indicating to the computer whether the command has been carried out. If so, the high-beam indicator light glows on the instrument panel. If not, a headlight-malfunction message might appear there. In addition, smart power can compensate for a missing high beam. In many cars, the low-beam filament is purposely extinguished when the high beam is selected. A smart-power system can be programmed to respond to a high-beam malfunction by lighting the low beam instead.

COMPUTERS TAKE WING
Conservatism as well as the cost of computers had much to do with the automobile industry's reluctance to design digital devices into the family car. As long as less expensive mechanical devices provided workable solutions to pollution and drivability problems, car manufacturers were happy to ignore computers.

This point of view was perhaps even more pronounced among builders of commercial aircraft, though it may seem out of character for a business that invented an autopilot in 1914 and, in the twenty-five years following World War II, had reduced the length of a cross-country journey by airliner from three days to five hours. Airlines had won the public's trust in the reliability and safety of air travel. So they reacted warily to the idea that aircraft might be computerized: Such innovations might threaten that hard-earned trust.

When computers at last began to make their way into civilian aircraft, they entered through the side door. Initially they were confined to areas of aircraft operation where a failure could not endanger the safety of the passengers and crew or the completion of a flight. By the mid-1960s, for example, aircraft technicians were using computerized data-collection systems to maintain the planes. The Airborne Integrated Data System collected information in flight about engines, generators, and other equipment. On the ground, the data helped maintenance crews detect poorly performing equipment before it stopped working altogether.

Flight crews first benefited from computers at about the same time, with the introduction of inertial navigation systems to commercial aircraft. This approach to finding a distant destination had already proved itself in some types of military aircraft and as a guidance system for missiles and rockets. In essence, an inertial guidance system detects the slightest change in a vehicle's speed or direction. From this information, a computer calculates how far and along what course the vehicle has progressed from its starting point, which is recorded with the system before takeoff as latitude and longitude (pages 58-59). Airline crews accepted inertial navigation in part because they were not totally dependent on the new technology. A doubting navigator had other means, including the venerable sextant, with which to establish the aircraft's position.

Engineer Dick Peal, who moved into the commercial aviation side of Boeing in 1966 after ten years of designing military electronics for the company, recalled briefing an airline executive on the advances being made in digital instruments by the manufacturers of aircraft avionics. "It was his very strong opinion," said Peal, "that any mass application of that technology to the air-transport industry was not going to happen because of the fact that the airlines were comfortable with what they had and because of the exposure that the application had to passenger safety."

As the trend toward digital systems inched forward, it became clear that the key to eventual acceptance of computer technology lay in successfully addressing what engineers call human factors, that is, how well the new instrument appealed to flight crews. Airplanes were flown by people who had developed a high degree of confidence not only in the instruments themselves but in their own ability to work with them—even in cases of extreme emergency.

THE INSTRUMENT PANEL REVISITED

At first, avionics engineers demonstrated digital instruments that looked unlike anything the aviators had used before. The all-important airspeed indicator, for example, was replaced with a kind of bar graph, in which the length of the bar showed the craft's airspeed. But pilots preferred the familiar to the unusual; they simply did not want a lengthening and shortening bar of light to replace the movement of a pointer around a dial.

Avionics firms believed they had the answer when, in the late 1960s, they developed a video display that reproduced conventional dials on a small television-like screen. Boeing installed these as well as a digital autopilot and navigation computer in a 737 jet and showed it to pilots.

The response was less than ecstatic. The reason, this time, was the issue of color rather than shape. Conventional instruments were boldly colored to show at a glance safe zones and danger zones of operation, such as high engine speed or low oil pressure. The actual numbers on a instrument were often no more significant than whether the instrument's pointer had settled solidly in the green range or was creeping toward the red. The digital instruments that Boeing so hopefully demonstrated in the 737 displayed their information in black and white, and not even clever use of contrasting grays could compensate for the vivid colors that they were intended to represent.

The breakthrough came without warning during a mid-1970s meeting of Boeing engineers, suppliers of digital displays, and representatives from instrument manufacturers and airlines at Boeing facilities in Renton, Washington. "We had set up in our theater," Peal recalled, "a place where each of the suppliers could put up his demonstrator to give our customer airlines, our suppliers, and ourselves a chance to look at all the systems."

Unbeknown to any of the other participants, one instrument maker, Collins Radio, had contracted with a Japanese company to provide them with a small color cathode-ray tube (CRT)—much like the one to be found in an ordinary color television set, except that this tube had been built to operate reliably when subjected to the rigors of flight. "They set up their demonstrator," said Peal, "and turned on this color tube. It was immediately obvious to the assembled pilots and engineers that here was a device that addressed the human-factor considerations."

Initially, efforts to pursue this development further were centered around the airspeed indicator, the altimeter, the artificial horizon, and other primary flight instruments. Soon, however, other applications for color CRTs became apparent. For example, engine instruments were integrated with caution and warning information into a system known as EICAS—Engine Indication and Caution Advisory System.

AIRLINERS THAT CAN FLY THEMSELVES

Along with Collins's watershed color display came the further computerization of the airliner. The autopilot and autothrottle systems—which until now had been based on analog technology—joined the ranks of microprocessor-based systems for commercial aircraft. Indeed, a system called the Flight Management Computer System (FMCS) had been installed in the 737 test-bed aircraft. FMCS's computer keeps track of every aspect of an airplane's performance, from airspeed and rate of descent to throttle setting and fuel consumption.

At the core of the system is a data base that contains a complete performance profile of the aircraft. In this data base resides detailed information on such topics as the maximum and minimum speeds at which the plane will fly, the amount of power required to maintain altitude, climb, or descend at various speeds, the effect of payload on performance, as well as facts about the aircraft's fuel consumption at different speeds and altitudes. The data base even contains the manual of emergency procedures for the aircraft. Should one of the engines fail, for example, the FMCS first alerts the pilot to the malfunction by signaling the caution advisory system to change the color of the appropriate engine instrument and to issue the proper visual warnings or cautions, some of which are accompanied by an aural signal. Automatically, the EICAS displays all the steps for dealing with the problem, from new power settings for the remaining engines to the procedure for restarting the dead one. In the case of multiple failures—the engine and the landing gear, for instance—the EICAS assigns priorities to each, so that the pilot can deal with the most critical emergency first.

An airline's route structure—airports, navigation aids between them, radio frequencies, and the like—can also be recorded in the FMCS data base. This enables the crew to program the computer with

most of the information needed to get an airliner to its destination—including special requirements such as the route to fly immediately after takeoff in order to conform to noise-abatement procedures in effect at particular airports, and details about the primary cross-country route and alternates. The computer can even be directed to automatically switch radio frequencies as necessary to enable the pilot to keep in contact with air-traffic controllers on the ground. If the plane's pilot wished to do so, he could program an entire flight, beginning with the takeoff roll, and would not have to touch the controls at all until after the aircraft had landed (except to obey unanticipated instructions from an air-traffic controller or perhaps to skirt a thunderstorm or two).

FMCS and EICAS, along with other computers aboard an aircraft, constitute an integrated flight-management system linked to all of an aircraft's vital controls, sensors, and instruments. Consequently, the computer can be programmed to keep the plane within the limits of safe flight. The system can also tell the pilot when failures or other problems keep it from performing this role, so that he can resume manual control of the plane.

Computerizing the Cockpit

1

Nowhere is the impact of computer technology on commercial aviation more apparent than in the cockpit of a modern jetliner. In Airbus Industrie's A320 *(left)*, the traditional control column, customarily positioned in front of the pilot and used to bank the plane and make it climb or descend, has been replaced by a simple but sophisticated control stick at the side of the cockpit. Dozens of dials and gauges have been supplanted by a handful of computer screens.

Different computer systems are responsible for each of these alterations in the pilot's office. In overall command are twin flight-management computers *(1)*, one of which serves as backup to the other. Before takeoff, the two-man crew uses either keyboard to enter the flight plan—altitudes, speeds, and intermediate destinations—simultaneously into both computers; the information is displayed on the small screen above each keyboard. After the plane is aloft, the computers take over, guiding the craft, constantly checking on its many complex systems, and feeding data to subsidiary computers.

Among the most important of these are the display-management computers, which control the instrument panel. Though a few standard instruments remain as backups, six computer screens supply all essential flight and performance information in easy-to-read formats. The Primary Flight Displays *(2)*, one each for pilot and copilot, do the work of several key instruments, showing the plane's attitude, heading, airspeed, and altitude. The Navigation Displays *(3)* present directional and routing information on a compass layout, and can also project a radar image of the weather. Two System Displays *(4 and 5)* provide continual updates on the functioning of the engines and other critical components; should a problem arise that the flight-management computers cannot handle, diagrams and checklists appear on these screens to guide the pilots through corrective procedures.

The two side sticks *(6)* are managed by another computer, part of the A320's fly-by-wire system. Stick movements are translated into electrical signals, thus eliminating the bulky mechanical connections of older designs. The approach prevents the pilot from ever overstressing the plane by maneuvering the stick too violently: Before the signals are relayed to control surfaces on the wings and tail, they pass through the fly-by-wire computer, which acts like a damper, moderating the most extreme gestures.

Computers have proved to be such excellent assistants on the flight deck that they have for several years permitted some commercial airliners to be flown by a crew of two instead of three, as required in the 1970s. Besides saving the third officer's salary, computers conserve fuel by flying a plane straighter than a human pilot can, improve the reliability of aircraft, and simplify the troubleshooting of malfunctioning equipment. Taken altogether, the economic benefits of computer-controlled flight-management systems have far exceeded the cost of installing them.

TRADING TUBES FOR WIRES

A few airplane builders have taken yet another step toward the fully computerized airliner by installing fly-by-wire control. In this system, digital signals instead of mechanical or hydraulic linkages transmit movements of the pilot's hands and feet to the aircraft's various control surfaces—ailerons on the wings for banking the plane, elevators at the tail to raise or lower the nose, and a rudder to help the aircraft turn. Developed by aeronautical engineers in the mid-1970s for high-performance combat aircraft like the F-16 fighter-bomber, the system has been built into the Airbus A320, an airliner produced by a consortium of European aircraft manufacturers.

In flying a conventional airliner, the pilot activates a pressure-driven hydraulic system that moves the flight surfaces. To climb, for example, he pulls back on the control column. This action moves a piston inside a cylinder attached to one end of a long fluid-filled tube that leads to a similar cylinder at the elevator. Depending on whether the control-column piston slides deeper into the cylinder or is partially withdrawn from it, fluid is pushed or pulled through the tube, causing the piston in the cylinder at the other end of the tube to move in or out. The result: The elevator pivots upward, causing the plane to climb. In this kind of control system, an autopilot moves control surfaces by

replacing the pilot's muscles with its own—either air pressure or electric motors.

The plumbing for such a system is almost unimaginably complex. Of the nearly 2,000 hours a year spent maintaining the average jet airliner, about 400 hours are devoted to the hydraulic-control system. In contrast, the wires of a fly-by-wire system are all but maintenance-free, and, should anything go awry with the computer, a substitute one can be quickly installed.

In a fly-by-wire system, pressure-sensitive devices are connected to a handle known as a side stick controller (it is mounted at the side of the cockpit) that replaces the control column between the pilot's legs. The rudder pedals are linked to other similar sensors. These instruments measure the force that the pilot applies to the controls and convert that force into an electrical signal. An analog-to-digital converter translates this signal into a sequence of ones and zeros and sends it to a computer. When the pilot pulls back on the controller in order to climb, the message to the flight-control computer is "lift elevators." The computer then instructs hydraulic actuators located on the tail of the plane to pivot the elevators a preprogrammed amount, proportional to the force exerted by the pilot through the side stick controller. The elevators lift, pointing the nose of the plane upward.

COMPUTERS AND SHIPS

Though humans have been airborne only since the beginning of the eighteenth century—first in balloons and later in airplanes—sailors have been going down to the sea in ships for 4,000 years, time enough to have established a seafaring tradition fully as conservative as any that aviators might have labored under. Yet seamen are an adventurous and pragmatic lot. They abandoned their coast-hugging ways when the compass and astrolabe made it possible to sail beyond sight of land. They gave up the cathedral beauty of sail for the gritty but certain power of coal; and, albeit gradually, they came to embrace the computer as a worthy mate.

Computers first proved themselves deep inside the engine room, where electronic sensors had long been used to send key information—engine speed, exhaust temperature, fuel flow, generator voltage output, and the like—to the ship's bridge. With this arrangement, fewer crew members were needed in the engine room to read gauges and dials, though someone had to closely monitor engine performance from the bridge. Early shipboard computers took over that responsibility. They accepted sensor data as input and compared it with ranges of normal values stored in memory. If, for example, the exhaust temperature climbed too high for engine-operating conditions, the computer printed a warning message. As computers assumed more and more responsibility in this arena, engine-room crews were eventually eliminated. Crewless engine rooms have resulted in substantial savings for ship operators with no compromise in safety.

Nowadays, shipboard computers not only monitor the engine and associated equipment, they control it as well. For example, they adjust the supply of electricity from a vessel's generators to the demand for electric power at a given moment. By taking unneeded generators off line, computers lengthen the useful life of this costly machinery and save fuel from being wasted in the production of excess power.

Sensors in a ship's hold provide data on the vessel's trim—its balance fore and aft and from side to side. Should the ship become bow-heavy, which can make it difficult to handle during heavy weather, or if the center of gravity rises too high, increasing the risk of capsizing, the computer immediately turns on pumps that redistribute fuel oil or sea-water ballast to restore balance to the ship. In order to save fuel and maintenance time, today's computers are even assigned the task of monitoring the amount of corrosion and barnacles fouling the ship's hull. To do this, the computer compares the ship's speed at various power settings with a performance data base established during the ship's sea trials, when the hull was clean.

THE RETURN TO SAIL

The computer's ability to integrate and oversee diverse functions has been instrumental in a return to the use of sail power. Commercial sailing died at the end of the nineteenth century, killed off by steamships that could pare the long run from England to the Orient by ten or fifteen days and operate on cheap, plentiful coal with far smaller, less costly crews. But in the late 1970s, when fuel became expensive, nautical engineers began to investigate whether wind power, coupled with computer technology, could brace the dwindling profits of merchant shipping.

Japan had particularly good reason to consider a return to sail. An island nation, Japan is dependent on seagoing vessels for trade even with such near neighbors as China and Taiwan. Furthermore, Japan's oil deposits are meager. In 1978, the Japanese Marine Machinery Development Association began research into the design and operation of a hybrid ship—one that would rely on sail to assist, rather than replace, power. The result would be a tanker christened *Shin Aitoku Maru*.

Six years behind the Japanese came Windstar Sail Cruises Limited, an American company formed in 1984 to build and operate a fleet of sail-powered luxury cruise ships—designed and built in France—for touring the islands of the Caribbean and the Pacific Ocean. "Our idea was not to save money," explained a Windstar official, "but to give a real sea vacation to passengers." Through technology, the company hoped to bring cruise passengers the charm and pleasure of sailing, "to expose the passenger to the beauty of the sights, the water, and the wind."

Development of the Japanese and French-built ships both began with computer models of the vessels. In the modeling, virtually every aspect of a ship that affects performance and that can be described mathematically is programmed into a computer. Some of the important factors are the vessel's length along the waterline, its beam, its displacement, detailed projections of hull contours, placement and height of masts, sail area, and even the rigging. The model also contains data about how water interacts with the ship's hull, and wind with the sails.

Heading the French team of naval architects who designed the first two cruise ships, the *Wind Star* and the *Wind Song,* was François Faury, a maritime engineer and manager of a large shipyard in the sprawling port of Le Havre. Faury had worked on the construction of France's first nuclear submarine and enjoyed being a pioneer of new technologies. Thus, he was pleasantly surprised at the challenges presented by the first of the two vessels, the *Wind Star*. "Many of the systems we needed were completely new," explained Faury of the ship's equipment, "and we had to develop them ourselves. This is especially true of the masts and rigging. To get the proper dimensions, such as thickness and height, we had to do a lot of tests."

The French experience was typical of modern ship-design practice, in which computers are essential. "We ran early tests on sails in a wind tunnel near Paris," notes Faury. "We would process the results of one test with our computers, learn what we needed to study further, then prepare the equipment for another test." When everything seemed in order, they built a one-twentieth-scale model of the ship and equipped it with electronic sensors to feed data to computers linked to a wind tunnel twenty-six feet in diameter, at Modane on the border between France and Italy. Owned by Onera, an aerodynamic research company, the tunnel cost so much to rent that Faury could afford to use it for only one week. But that was all the time needed to refine and complete the sail design and to write simulation software, which would later become the programs that would run the ship. The week at Onera was so successful that when the software was tested on the actual ship, there were only a few minor bugs to work out.

SAILS FOR THE NEW SEAMANSHIP
A striking difference between the French luxury cruise ship and the Japanese tanker lies in the shapes of their sails. The *Shin Aitoku Maru*, designed expressly to reduce the cost of importing petroleum by sea, has two rigid sails, forty feet high and twenty-six feet wide, made of an open steel framework covered with canvas. When unfolded to the wind, the sails resemble those that powered square riggers of the nineteenth century and earlier, though they are much more effective. No ship can sail directly upwind, but the *Shin Aitoku Maru* can make headway under sail headed as close as twenty degrees to the wind; most square riggers could sail no closer than sixty degrees to the wind. The *Wind Star*, the better to enhance the sensations of sailing for its passengers, has cloth sails, huge triangles of Dacron with an area exceeding 21,000 square feet. Stretched tautly by the wind, they are capable of moving the 440-foot-long ship at twelve knots.

Instead of relying on sailors, captains of both ships depend on the brain power of computers and the muscle of hydraulic actuators to set and furl the sails. Aboard the *Wind Star* and the *Wind Song,* sensors provide information about the angle of each sail, the position of each boom, and of course, wind speed and direction. A minicomputer in a small room behind the bridge compares the information with a performance profile of the ship loaded into memory. Pro-

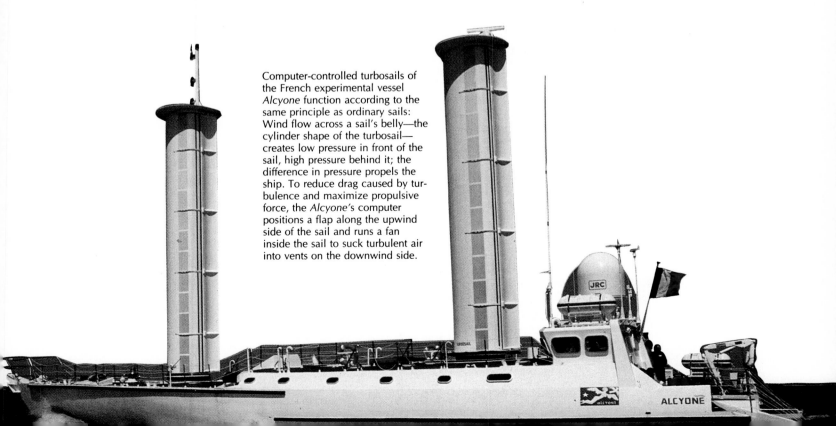

Computer-controlled turbosails of the French experimental vessel *Alcyone* function according to the same principle as ordinary sails: Wind flow across a sail's belly—the cylinder shape of the turbosail—creates low pressure in front of the sail, high pressure behind it; the difference in pressure propels the ship. To reduce drag caused by turbulence and maximize propulsive force, the *Alcyone*'s computer positions a flap along the upwind side of the sail and runs a fan inside the sail to suck turbulent air into vents on the downwind side.

grammed with software that has been fine-tuned so that the ship achieves the maximum speed possible for any wind conditions, the computer analyzes the data, displays the position of all booms and sails on a color screen on the bridge, and issues the appropriate commands to hydraulic systems that operate the sails.

Computers control the sails of the *Shin Aitoku Maru* in a similar fashion, but the Japanese tanker also has what amounts to a seagoing cruise control that employs sail power to reduce the amount of engine power needed to keep on schedule. The system consists of several computers. A trim computer communicates information about the weight of the ship's load to a navigation computer, into which the ship's master enters the distance to the next port, the time he wishes to arrive there, and information on currents and winds to be encountered on the voyage. The result is the speed that the ship must make in order to reach its destination on schedule. When the vessel is under way, the captain accelerates under diesel power to the correct speed. A load-control computer notes how much power the engine is producing to maintain this speed, then, after the sail-management computer has spread the sails, automatically throttles back the engine according to the amount of power being contributed by the wind.

Just as computers have proved economical in automobiles as pollution-control managers, to name but one automotive role, and in airliners as a multitalented crew member that can be trusted with the safety of plane and passengers, computers have also demonstrated their value in commercial shipping. For the *Shin Aitoku Maru,* fuel savings over conventionally powered ships are estimated to be as much as 50 percent, and fifteen other sail-assisted ships have joined the fleet. The ships of Windstar Sail Cruises have been just as satisfying in their own terms. Not only do they share the fuel efficiency of the Japanese tankers, burning 40 to 50 percent less diesel oil than comparable ships having no sails, but they have proved their appeal in the competitive vacation market. So prosperous have the ships made Windstar Sail Cruises that a third sister ship, the *Wind Spirit,* is set to offer well-heeled vacationers cruises under sail to other exotic ports of call.

The Car
Goes Digital

The automobile of the late twentieth century is a technological hybrid that Henry Ford would have marveled at—a sophisticated blend of mechanics and electronics. Virtually all cars that are made in the world today have onboard microprocessors. Originally developed to help cars meet government standards for fuel efficiency and emission control, automotive computers now perform a wide range of tasks, from improving handling and stability to creating a more comfortable environment for the occupants.

In a so-called smart car, microprocessors are separately assigned to oversee and assist different mechanical systems, such as the engine, the brakes, or the suspension; their circuits are programmed to recognize certain conditions and take appropriate action in response. Essential to the process is a constant supply of information about operating conditions and the particular system's performance. An extensive network of sensors provides that input, transmitting data as electrical signals for the computers to analyze. Completing their calculations at lightning speed, the computers then fire off instructions to actuators—electronically controlled devices such as motors, pumps, and valves—to effect the necessary adjustments. Corrections occur continuously, producing an unparalleled level of fine-tuning.

All this electronic activity calls for wiring throughout the car, which means added weight and an increased chance of something going wrong. Designers, however, have minimized the problem through multiplexing, the same technique used to transmit many telephone conversations over a single cable. Signals from several sensors are combined and travel together over one transmission line; the receiving computer unscrambles the messages, analyzes the data, and—in the space of perhaps a thousandth of a second—makes decisions that will keep the car working its best.

A Gallery of Sensors

Without effective sensors, even the most powerful computers could do little to improve an automobile's performance. Although they vary in design and purpose, the many different sensing devices in a computerized car all perform the same basic function: They translate physical phenomena into electrical signals, thereby supplying the information computers need in a form they can understand.

The illustrations below show six of the most common automotive sensors; color-coded insets on the larger drawing at

Rotation sensor. Designed to record the rate at which something spins, this sensor consists of two separate components: a toothed metal disk mounted on the revolving part and a stationary detector that houses a magnetic coil, through which current passes. As the teeth move past the coil, they disturb its magnetic field, generating a stream of pulses in the current. The computer calculates rotational speed from the frequency of the pulses.

Position sensor. This sensor indicates the location of a moving part by varying the resistance in an electrical circuit. The computer sends a reference current through a circuit formed by a contact needle that pivots over a resistor *(zigzag wire)*. Movement by the part sweeps the needle either left or right, altering the circuit's resistance and thus the current returning to the computer. As the needle moves left, for example, the current passes through more of the resistor, and the return flow decreases in proportion.

Temperature sensor. The temperature of a gas or a liquid can also be communicated electronically through variations in a circuit's resistance. Again, the computer supplies a reference current to a circuit within the sensor, but the resistor is now a small piece of semiconductor material *(black square)* whose resistance varies with the temperature. Thus, changes in temperature either increase or decrease the current returning as a signal to the computer.

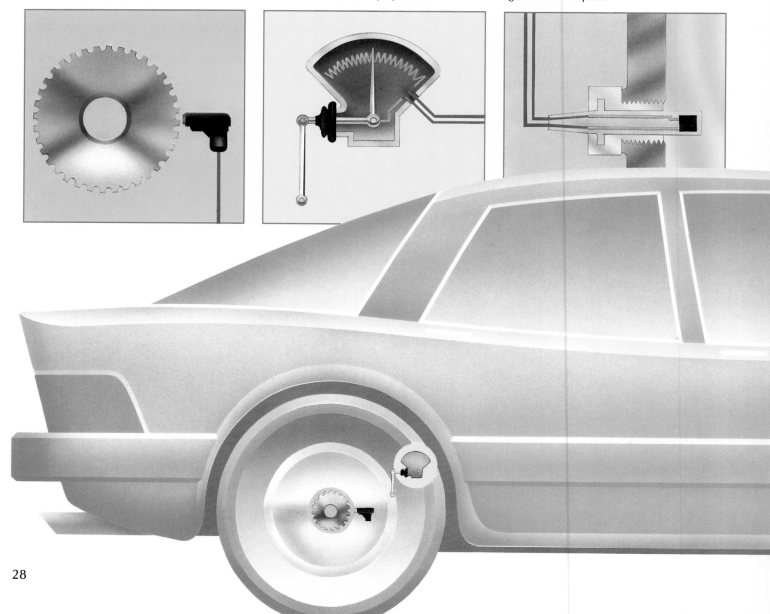

bottom indicate standard locations. Because they are designed to suit a variety of applications, some types of sensors, such as the three at left, are found in several different places. Rotation sensors, for example, not only measure the rate at which each wheel turns but also monitor the revolutions of the engine crankshaft *(pages 30-31)*. Position sensors detect everything from the height of the suspension system, as shown here, to the steering angle or the position of the throttle. And temperature sensors check on both liquids, such as engine coolant, and gases such as the air that is used in combustion or ventilation.

Other types of measurements require sensors like the three at right, each carefully crafted to serve one specific purpose. More sophisticated and complex in design than their general-purpose counterparts, these specialists provide computers with essential feedback about some of the more intricate processes related to the efficient functioning of the automobile's engine.

Airflow sensor. This sensor measures the air fed to the engine through the intake manifold. A small stream of air is diverted past two coiled wires; the first measures the air temperature, and the second is heated by the computer to a fixed level above that temperature. As rushing air cools the second wire, its resistance decreases. The computer detects the change and boosts the current to that wire, restoring it to the right temperature and resistance. The amount of current the computer must provide indicates the rate of flow.

Knock sensor. Engine knock occurs when fuel burns unevenly, causing irregular vibration in the engine. The knock sensor consists of an electric coil surrounding two ceramic rods and a magnet *(black square)*. Engine vibration in turn makes the rods vibrate, which disturbs the coil's magnetic field and alters the current passing through the coil and returning to the computer as a signal. The computer analyzes the signal pattern to determine whether the vibrations are characteristic of knocking.

Oxygen sensor. Inserted into the exhaust manifold, the oxygen sensor is a hollow tube divided into inner and outer compartments by a U-shaped, platinum-coated rod. Exhaust gas enters the outer compartment through a series of slits; the inner compartment is open to air through a vent at the other end. The platinum generates an electrical signal in response to the differing oxygen content on either side of the rod. The signal's strength tells the computer how much oxygen there is in the exhaust and thus how well the fuel is burning.

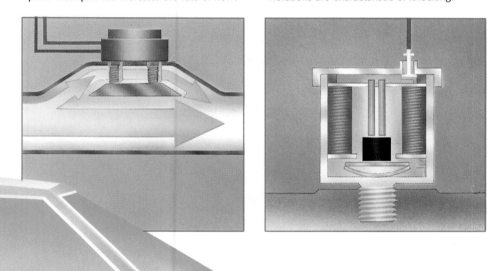

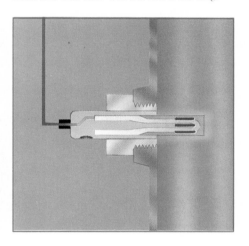

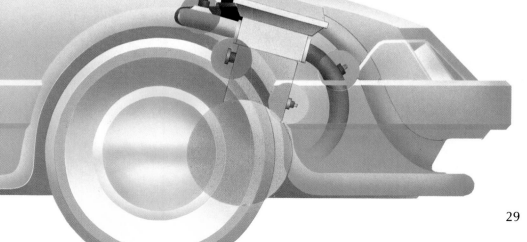

Getting the Most from the Engine

By far the most prominent role played by automotive computers is regulating the car's engine to optimize performance and at the same time improve both fuel economy and pollution control. The advent of electronics has come at the expense of two venerable engine components—the carburetor and the distributor—both rapidly disappearing from the automotive world.

One of the most important factors in engine performance

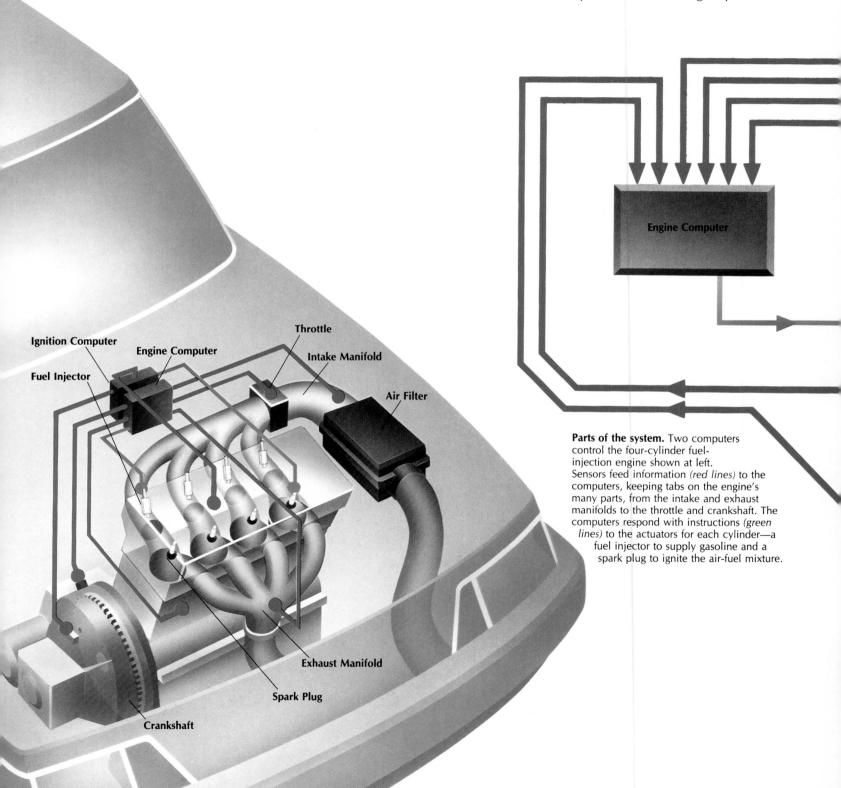

Ignition Computer

Engine Computer

Fuel Injector

Throttle

Intake Manifold

Air Filter

Engine Computer

Exhaust Manifold

Spark Plug

Crankshaft

Parts of the system. Two computers control the four-cylinder fuel-injection engine shown at left. Sensors feed information *(red lines)* to the computers, keeping tabs on the engine's many parts, from the intake and exhaust manifolds to the throttle and crankshaft. The computers respond with instructions *(green lines)* to the actuators for each cylinder—a fuel injector to supply gasoline and a spark plug to ignite the air-fuel mixture.

is proper mixing of fuel and air for combustion; the optimum ratio varies according to operating conditions, such as the temperature of the engine or the amount of throttle being applied. A carburetor adjusts the mixture mechanically, and it is less than precise. In most new cars, however, the job is done by a system called fuel injection, which works in tandem with a computer that calibrates the mixture with exquisite precision on a cylinder-by-cylinder basis.

A computer has also assumed control of ignition—the firing of the spark plugs. In older designs, the spinning of a rotor in a distributor dispersed current in sequence to each of the plugs. An ignition computer, on the other hand, regulates each plug individually. Thus, should one plug misfire, the computer can fine-tune the timing to coordinate the actions of all the pistons. Such independent control virtually guarantees a more efficient production of power.

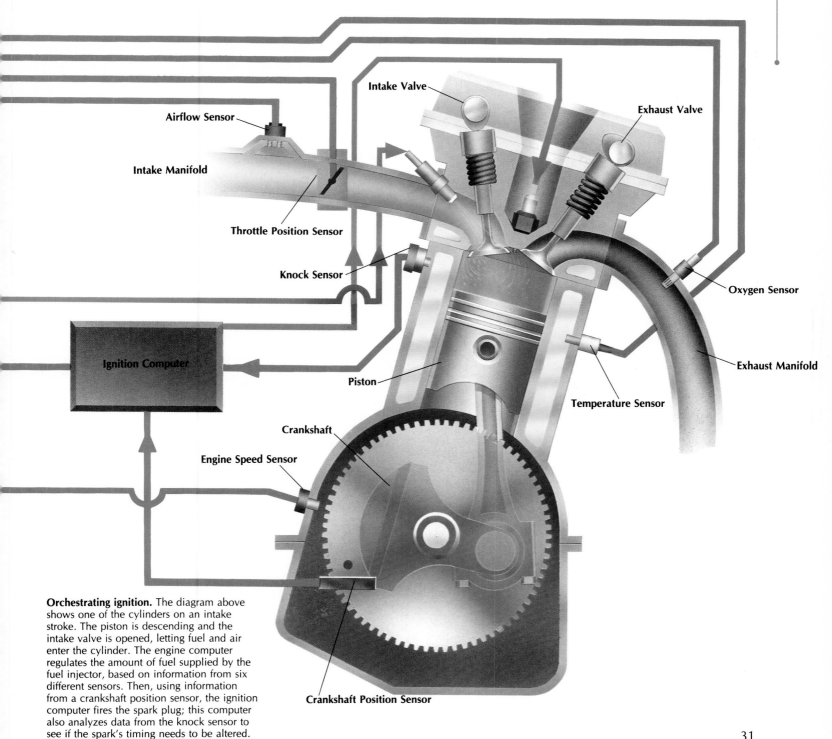

Orchestrating ignition. The diagram above shows one of the cylinders on an intake stroke. The piston is descending and the intake valve is opened, letting fuel and air enter the cylinder. The engine computer regulates the amount of fuel supplied by the fuel injector, based on information from six different sensors. Then, using information from a crankshaft position sensor, the ignition computer fires the spark plug; this computer also analyzes data from the knock sensor to see if the spark's timing needs to be altered.

31

Steering with All Four Wheels

Four-wheel steering, a feature of some new cars, represents a dramatic improvement in handling over the conventional front-wheels-only approach. And properly coordinating the actions of the front and rear wheels is a task ideally suited to the precision monitoring and control a computer can offer.

At speeds of more than about twenty miles per hour, an automobile's front-wheel-steering computer ensures that

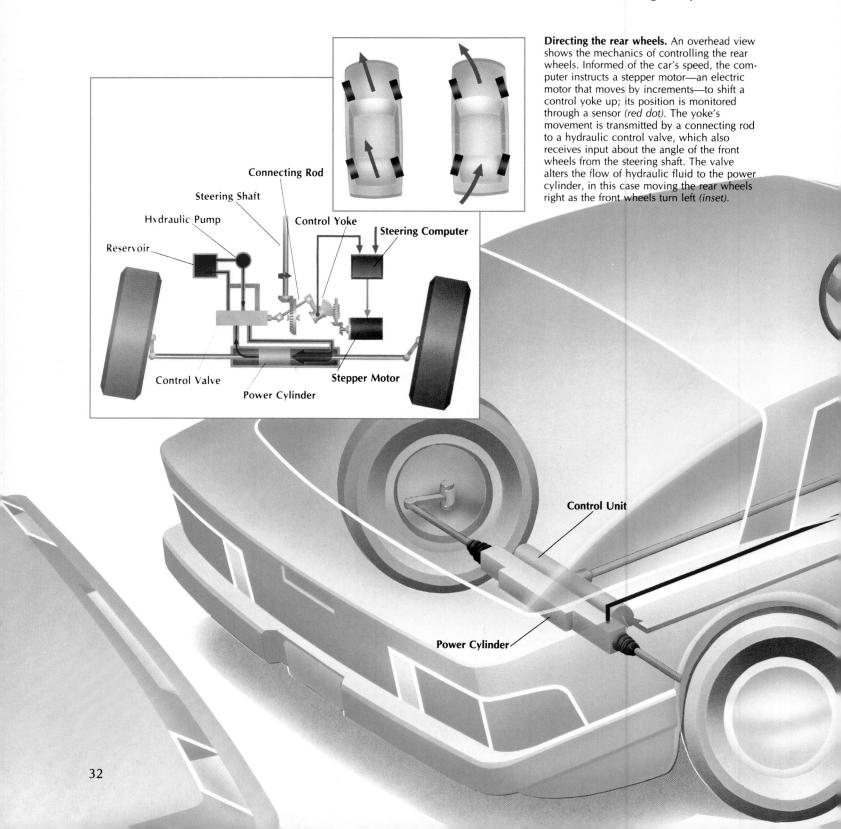

Directing the rear wheels. An overhead view shows the mechanics of controlling the rear wheels. Informed of the car's speed, the computer instructs a stepper motor—an electric motor that moves by increments—to shift a control yoke up; its position is monitored through a sensor *(red dot)*. The yoke's movement is transmitted by a connecting rod to a hydraulic control valve, which also receives input about the angle of the front wheels from the steering shaft. The valve alters the flow of hydraulic fluid to the power cylinder, in this case moving the rear wheels right as the front wheels turn left *(inset)*.

Connecting Rod

Steering Shaft

Hydraulic Pump

Control Yoke

Steering Computer

Reservoir

Control Valve

Power Cylinder

Stepper Motor

Control Unit

Power Cylinder

both sets of wheels turn in the same direction *(inset opposite, left)*. Because the rear wheels contribute to the maneuver rather than pointing straight ahead and being, in effect, dragged through the curve, stability is enhanced. At lower speeds, however, the rear wheels are directed to turn opposite to the front wheels *(inset opposite, right)*, which reduces the car's turning radius, thus improving maneuverability in city traffic, for example, and making it much simpler to squeeze into narrow parking places.

Through a complex system of gears *(opposite)*, the computer changes not only the direction of rear-wheel movement but the degree of movement as well. Stability is maximized if a turn of the steering wheel moves the rear wheels less at high speeds than it does at lower speeds.

Synchronized steering. Four-wheel steering combines a hydraulic steering system with computer control. Hydraulic fluid *(purple)* is pumped to power cylinders for both the front and the rear wheels to move them either right or left. The steering wheel controls the front wheels, but a steering computer determines whether the rear wheels will turn with the front ones or in the opposite direction, depending on how fast the car is traveling. The computer receives input *(red)* from a vehicle speed sensor at the transmission and sends its instructions *(green)* to a control unit for the rear wheels.

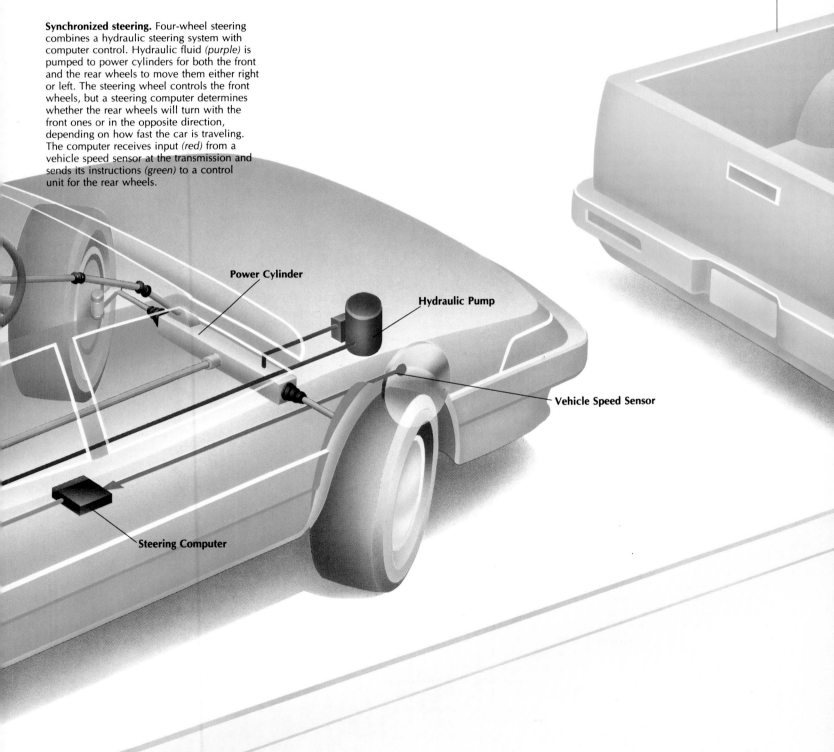

Power Cylinder

Hydraulic Pump

Vehicle Speed Sensor

Steering Computer

Adjusting the Shocks on the Go

Road conditions can vary tremendously in the course of a journey, from the city's bumps and potholes to the highway's smooth paving. Under the control of a computer, a smart car's suspension can adapt to these changes, continuously working out the best compromise of stability and comfort.

As always, sensors are crucial to the computer's responsiveness. By reporting on the action of each wheel's suspen-

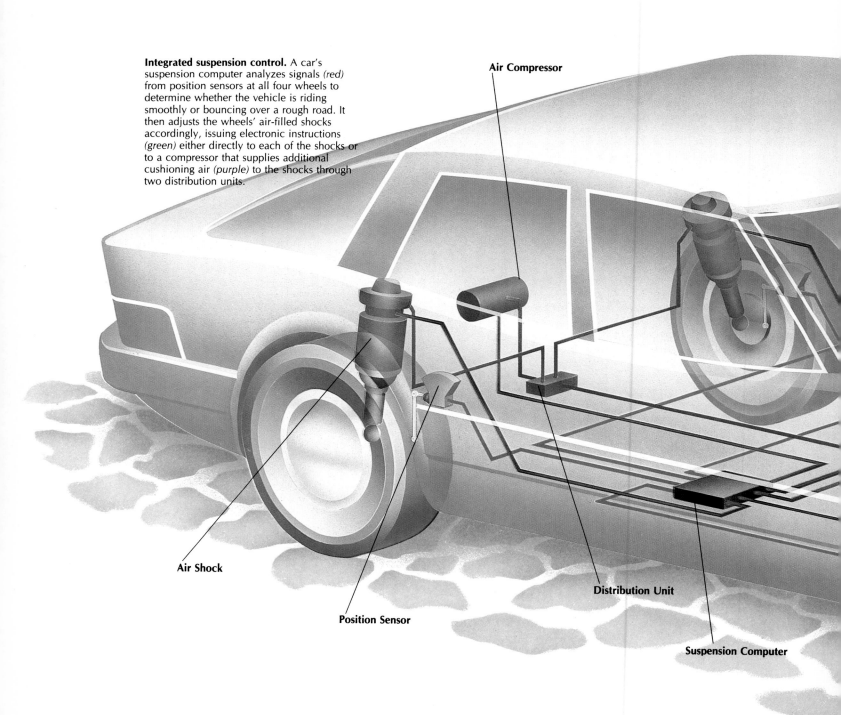

Integrated suspension control. A car's suspension computer analyzes signals *(red)* from position sensors at all four wheels to determine whether the vehicle is riding smoothly or bouncing over a rough road. It then adjusts the wheels' air-filled shocks accordingly, issuing electronic instructions *(green)* either directly to each of the shocks or to a compressor that supplies additional cushioning air *(purple)* to the shocks through two distribution units.

Air Compressor

Air Shock

Position Sensor

Distribution Unit

Suspension Computer

sion, they enable the computer to judge the surface the car is traveling on at any given moment. The computer can then alter the give in the shock absorbers to match the conditions. If the surface is rough, for example, the shocks are stiffened, which enables them to absorb the bumpiness without jarring the frame of the car itself. But on smooth surfaces, the shocks are softened, producing more of a luxury-car feel; occasional small bumps are completely cushioned by the extra give, and the car body remains steady.

In similar fashion, the computer can adjust each shock individually to compensate for uneven distribution of weight in the car. With the trunk fully loaded, for instance, the rear end would sit lower, but by pumping up the rear shocks, the computer automatically keeps the car frame on an even keel.

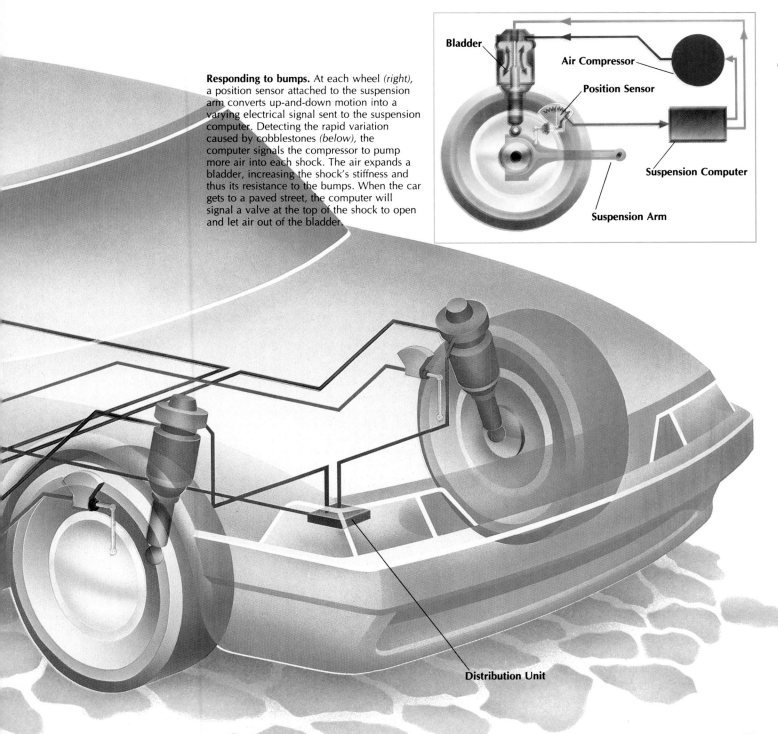

Responding to bumps. At each wheel (right), a position sensor attached to the suspension arm converts up-and-down motion into a varying electrical signal sent to the suspension computer. Detecting the rapid variation caused by cobblestones (below), the computer signals the compressor to pump more air into each shock. The air expands a bladder, increasing the shock's stiffness and thus its resistance to the bumps. When the car gets to a paved street, the computer will signal a valve at the top of the shock to open and let air out of the bladder.

Bladder

Air Compressor

Position Sensor

Suspension Computer

Suspension Arm

Distribution Unit

Assisting the Brakes Electronically

Perhaps the most important safety innovation in a computerized car is its antilock braking system (ABS), which helps prevent skidding during sudden stops. On a wet or even a snowy road, the computer's fine-tuned management of the brakes allows the driver to maintain control of the car all the way to a complete stop.

Wheel lock often occurs in panic situations, when the

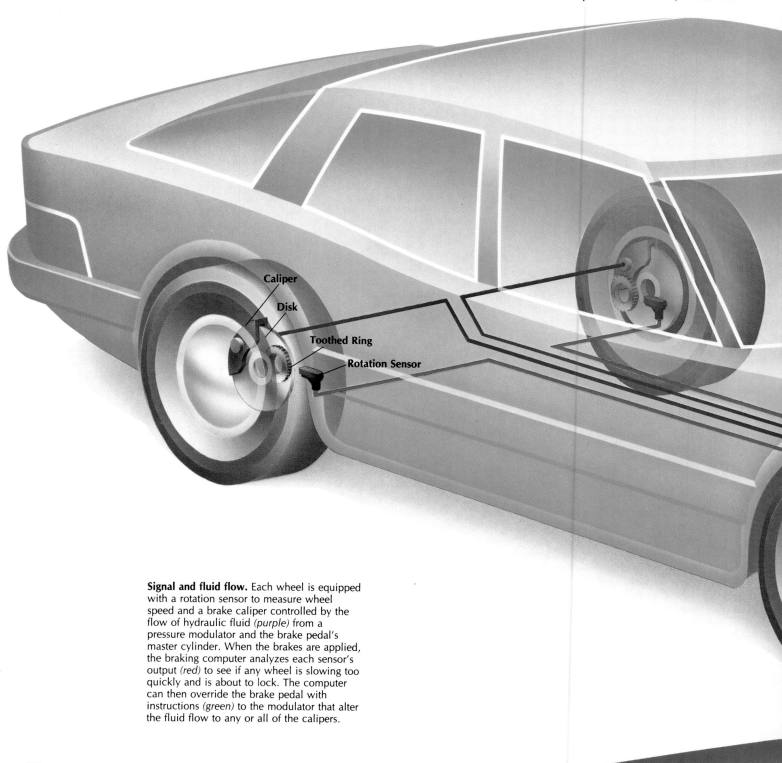

Caliper

Disk

Toothed Ring

Rotation Sensor

Signal and fluid flow. Each wheel is equipped with a rotation sensor to measure wheel speed and a brake caliper controlled by the flow of hydraulic fluid *(purple)* from a pressure modulator and the brake pedal's master cylinder. When the brakes are applied, the braking computer analyzes each sensor's output *(red)* to see if any wheel is slowing too quickly and is about to lock. The computer can then override the brake pedal with instructions *(green)* to the modulator that alter the fluid flow to any or all of the calipers.

driver slams on the brakes in an effort to stop the car as quickly as possible. Applying too much pressure to the brakes too suddenly, especially on slick surfaces, can cause one or more of the wheels to stop rotating even though the car is still moving. The tires then become more like skis than wheels, and the car slides uncontrollably in the direction of its momentum, no matter which way the driver turns the steering wheel.

In an ABS-equipped car, however, the system pumps the brakes up to ten times a second—far faster than any human can achieve—whenever the computer senses that wheel lock is imminent. The split-second releases of pressure, regulated independently for each brake, keep the wheels turning even as they are slowed, and the driver retains the ability to guide the car out of trouble.

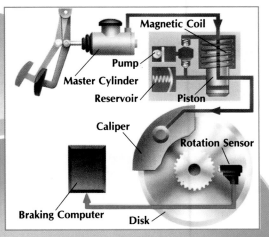
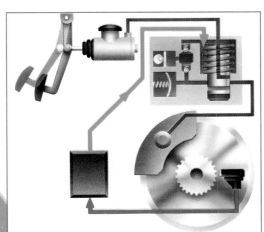
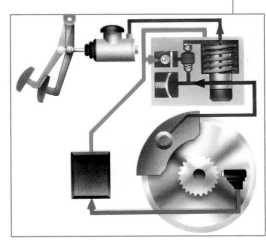

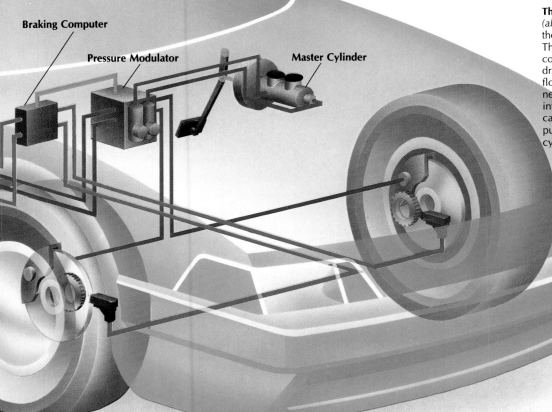

The pumping cycle. Stepping on the brake *(above, left)* forces fluid through a piston to the caliper, which squeezes the brake disk. The sensor indicates too-rapid slowing, so the computer sends current to a magnetic coil, drawing the piston up and cutting off the fluid flow *(center)*. As the piston rises farther, a new channel is opened, and fluid escapes into a reservoir, relieving pressure on the caliper *(right)*; the computer also operates a pump to send fluid back to the master cylinder. The cycle is then ready to repeat.

Computerized Comfort

In addition to improving the performance and safety of a car, computers help provide a more comfortable environment for a vehicle's occupants. The same kind of precision monitoring and control that computers apply to the functioning of the engine or the brakes serves equally well when it comes to adjusting the driver's seat or regulating the temperature inside the car.

A computer-controlled seat automatically adjusts to suit the

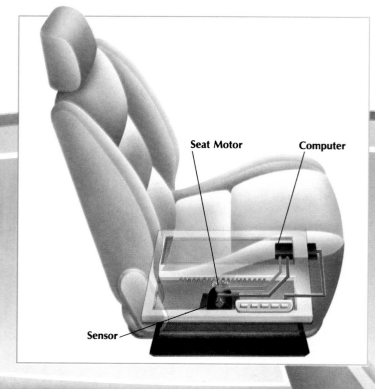

Seat Motor   **Computer**

Sensor

Moving the seat. To adjust the seat forward or backward, the driver pushes the far right-hand control button, which sends a signal *(red)* to the computer. The computer then supplies current *(green)* to the seat motor until the desired position is reached. A sensor in the motor returns a signal to the computer *(red)* that indicates how much current was required. Later, to set the same position after a change, another button is pushed, and the computer supplies current up to the level recorded in its memory.

preference of two different drivers by matching preselected settings. For clarity, the drawing at left illustrates only how the seat is moved forward and backward; in reality, its height and the position of the reclining back would be adjusted in a similar fashion. The computer is also programmed to move the seat back whenever the ignition is turned off, thus enabling the driver to exit more easily.

The chief advantage of a computerized climate-control system is its ability to adapt to circumstances automatically. On cold days, for example, the computer turns on front and rear defrosters as soon as the car is started. When the engine is warm, the heater is activated and the blower fan is turned on high until the desired temperature is reached. The system can even compensate for the extra radiant heat through the windshield on a sunny day, detected by one of two inside temperature sensors (below).

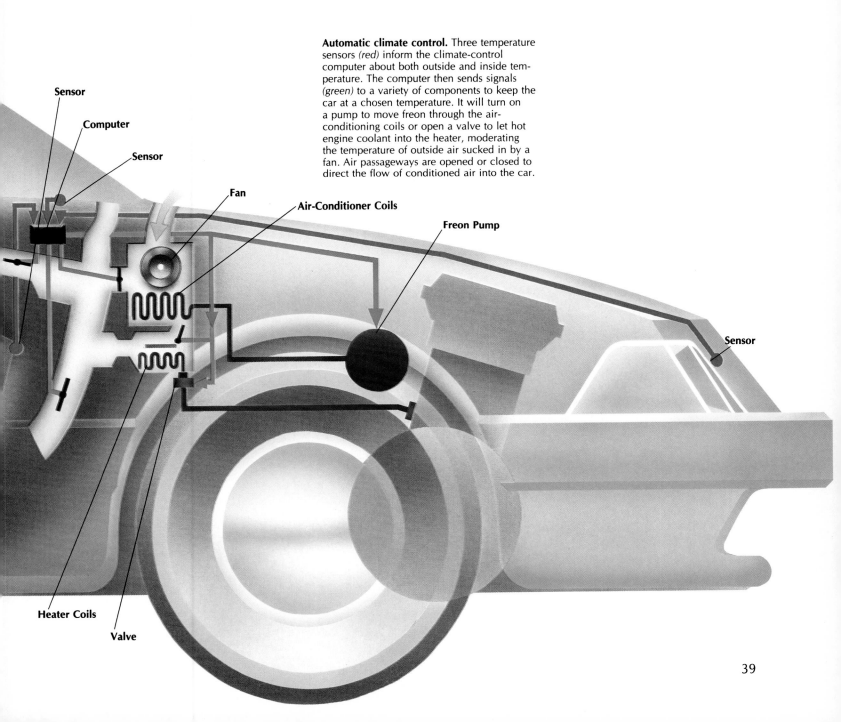

Automatic climate control. Three temperature sensors (red) inform the climate-control computer about both outside and inside temperature. The computer then sends signals (green) to a variety of components to keep the car at a chosen temperature. It will turn on a pump to move freon through the air-conditioning coils or open a valve to let hot engine coolant into the heater, moderating the temperature of outside air sucked in by a fan. Air passageways are opened or closed to direct the flow of conditioned air into the car.

Sensor

Computer

Sensor

Fan

Air-Conditioner Coils

Freon Pump

Sensor

Heater Coils

Valve

Keeping the Driver Informed

The several computer systems explained on the previous pages make use of a wide variety of information provided by sensors. In a smart car, a good deal of that information is also relayed to the driver through the car's instrument computer. This computer not only reports such standard readings as the vehicle's speed and fuel level but plays a diagnostic role as well: By constantly monitoring all the other computers and

A wealth of data. The dashboard of a computerized car combines traditional needle gauges and liquid crystal displays—all run by the instrument computer. Above the tachometer *(left)* and speedometer *(right),* a message screen alerts the driver to malfunctions, such as the failure of a sensor. Amber warning lights for the braking, steering, and suspension computers indicate if any of these systems are not working properly. Other computer-driven displays show the temperature of the car's interior, trip information, and radio tuning *(opposite).*

their components, it can give the driver early warning when something goes wrong.

The instrument computer projects all sorts of messages on its liquid crystal displays *(below)*. Programmed to keep track of the car's maintenance schedule, for example, it will tell the driver when to change the oil or replace the spark plugs. A trip information system, controlled by buttons on the dash, displays up-to-the-minute data on fuel consumption, how far the car can travel before running out of gas, and estimated time of arrival at a destination.

Computerized navigation systems are also becoming available, showing local maps and preferred routes to a destination. Steering and speed sensors help the computer track the car's location from a starting point indicated by the driver.

Information flow. The diagram below shows how information flows from the various system computers to the instrument computer, and finally to the dashboard display. The ignition computer reports through the engine computer, supplying details on such functions as the timing of the spark plugs. The engine computer also passes data to the instrument computer on engine temperature and speed, oil pressure, and the state of its sensors. The instrument computer processes information from all the systems, then adjusts needle gauges accordingly and delivers easy-to-understand messages to the display screens.

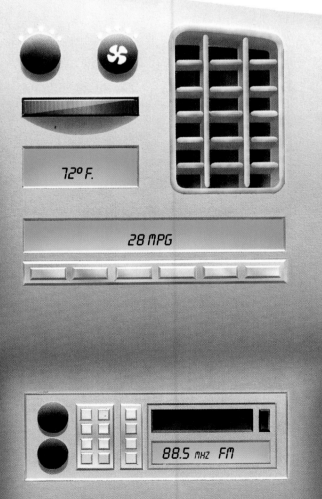

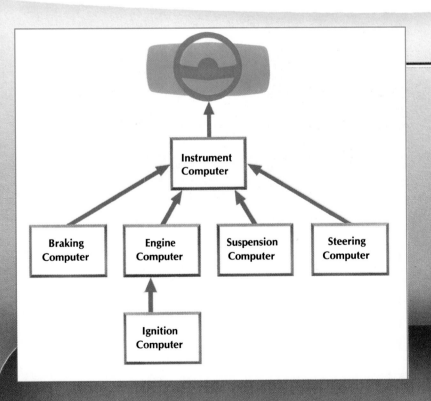

Electronic Wayfinding

Within the blink of a few decades in the middle of the twentieth century, computerized navigational techniques have almost completely supplanted the pathfinding methods that explorers and other travelers depended on for hundreds of years. Rendered obsolete, for the most part, were the sextant, chronometer, and star chart traditionally used by wayfarers to determine latitude and longitude and to track their passages through hazardous zones. The passing of these tools has diminished the need for highly trained navigation specialists versed in the techniques and mathematics required to use them. Now, with little effort, voyagers at sea, on land, and in the air can rely on computerized systems to steer sure, accurate courses.

Like their low-tech predecessors, such navigation systems can be grouped into two broad categories. One, known as dead reckoning, relies on instruments and sensors that are carried on the vehicle itself; by recording the distance and direction traveled from a known place of origin, these instruments make it possible to calculate the vehicle's present position. In the second category are systems that resort to outside agents to obtain a position fix. By using direct measurements of the angle or the distance to an object whose exact location is known, the instruments allow the determination of the vehicle's position relative to that location.

In the days of sail, a navigator's tools for dead reckoning were the compass for direction finding, and a variety of simple devices for determining speed. The most common speedometer was a log or wood chip tied to a knotted rope. The wood was dropped into the water and the rope allowed to play out freely; by counting the number of knots that ran out in a measured period of time, the navigator could tell how fast the ship was moving and thus calculate how far it had gone. By knowing how long the ship had traveled at a given speed in a given direction, the navigator could tell roughly where the vessel was in relation to its last known or calculated position. Modern dead reckoning connects a computer to instruments that monitor speed and direction; computed positions are always available at a moment's notice.

Sailors of the past could obtain external fixes while the ship was in sight of land by simultaneously taking the bearings of two or more landmarks; the ship's position would be at the point on a chart where the bearing lines crossed. Once the vessel was well at sea, celestial navigation became the primary method for checking position. This method involved using a sextant to measure the angle above the horizon of the sun, or of stars, planets, or the moon, at a precisely recorded time. The navigator could then employ special astronomical tables and mathematical formulas to determine where the ship was. With a good sextant and chronometer, the position might be accurate to within a mile or less. These techniques have been supplanted in many modern ships by radio navigation systems. Typically, a receiver on a vessel picks up radio signals from transmitters whose exact whereabouts are already known; the transmission may come from antennae on land or from navigational satellites circling high above the earth. In either case, a computer in the receiving equipment processes information from the signals to elicit the vessel's position.

NIGHT PASSAGE TO NORMANDY

As in many other areas of applied science, the Second World War spurred the development of electronic position finding and heralded the dawn of computerized navigation. The war in Europe was moving toward a thunderous climax in 1944 as the Allied forces prepared for a massive air and sea invasion of German-occupied France. The naval arm of this assault was to involve 8,000 vessels of all types that would ferry hundreds of thousands of troops across the English Channel.

Of the many perils the huge armada faced, the most immediate came from German mines—explosive canisters moored below the surface of the sea. Thousands of these mines, each capable of sinking a troop-laden ship, had been sowed in a great swath directly across the intended path of the invasion fleet. The task of clearing and marking narrow passages through the deadly tract of water for the first wave of transport ships fell to a flotilla of Royal Navy minesweepers. Not only would these small vessels have to find and detonate mines, but their night navigation also would have to be nearly perfect. A landfall error of even two hundred yards could be ruinous; carefully rehearsed soldiers in the first wave would find themselves landing on the wrong beaches, and the meticulously organized supply operation behind them could become hopelessly snarled. Moreover, this feat of navigation would not be performed in the narrow part of the Channel made famous by long-distance swimmers; for strategic reasons, the target was Normandy, ninety-two fog-ridden, current-swept miles from the south coast of England.

Just a few weeks before the scheduled invasion, minesweeper navigators were quietly introduced to the Royal Navy's answer to the challenge—the Blue Gasmeter Job. Such bizarre labels for military hardware were common at a time when security demanded that nothing ever be spoken of by its real name. Officially designated the QM, the device was the first operational version of one of the earliest radio navigational aids, the Decca Navigator. Its nickname was inspired by the blue enamel finish on the shipboard receivers, which with their two indicator dials did look a bit like gas meters.

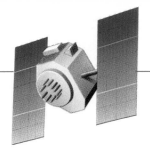

Although a similar radio system was already in use to help guide Allied bombers to their targets, the nautical Decca was kept under wraps until the eve of the invasion to avoid alerting the Germans, who might try to jam its signals. As part of the system, a set of three radio antennae carefully positioned along the south coast of England would transmit low-frequency signals; receiving units aboard the minesweepers would register the difference in the arrival time of these signals. The ships' navigators were issued charts overlaid with a so-called QM lattice, a fine web of crisscrossing lines, each corresponding to a time difference as indicated by one of the dials on the receiver. A navigator could determine his position at any time by finding the intersection of the two lattice lines indicated by the dials.

At 11 o'clock on the morning of June 5—D-Day minus one—the lead minesweeper weighed anchor behind the Isle of Wight, steamed past the chalk cliffs known as The Needles, and entered the open Channel. The following ships already were threatening to overrun the minesweeper; they all had started a little too soon, hoping to gain a few minutes against unforeseen developments. Manned for the most part by inexperienced reservists, the landing ships were difficult enough to handle in calm seas, let alone in the gale-churned Channel. Aboard the lead minesweeper, Lt. Comdr. Oliver Dawkins, the ship's navigator, felt his responsibility keenly. "Everything had to depend on accurate navigation and timing," Dawkins remembered. "If our row of buoys was straight and marked a clear, safe channel, it would make life a little easier for them the next morning."

The fleet sorted itself out and the minesweepers turned south toward France exactly on schedule. In his chart house, Dawkins watched the Decca indicator dials, comparing their readings with his charts and with dead-reckoning positions relayed from the wheelhouse. Soon the Gasmeter told him that the tidal current was edging the ship to the east; he called up a new course to the captain on the bridge. Night fell, and the ships began to encounter mines. The minesweepers cut their anchor cables and detonated them harmlessly. Further Decca readings indicated that the tide was running stronger than expected; Dawkins made additional course corrections. For fifteen hours, through a complete tidal cycle and several abrupt course reversals required to sweep the area of mines, the Gasmeter unerringly guided the flotilla to its destination, four miles off the coast of Normandy. At 3:25 in the morning of June 6, the preliminary bombardment began. Dawkins made a final check of his dials, then paid his first visit to the bridge since leaving England. "We had found the right beach, our troops would go ashore at the right spot," he exulted. "This moment in time was mine, never to be lost. A feeling that victory was certain, that nothing could stop that great flood of men and machines."

CREDIT TO THE BACKROOM BOYS

Dawkins and his peers recognized the debt they owed to the developers of the Decca Navigator. Those scientists and engineers, known to the combat troops as the backroom boys, had spent years perfecting the technology that smoothed the way on D-Day. Two other radio navigational systems, dubbed Gee and Loran, also blossomed in the forced-growth atmosphere of the back rooms and were pressed into operational duty. Like the Decca Navigator, these systems relied on the hyperbolic method of position fixing, using timing differences from signals of known origin. But in contrast to the Decca system, they employed radio beacons that sent out intermittent pulses rather than a steady stream of signals. One advantage that Gee and Loran had over Decca was that such pulsed signals were relatively immune to enemy jamming. In their early incarnations, however, they lacked the accuracy afforded by Decca.

Introduced in 1940, Gee was a British system custom-built to help guide the bombers based in England on raids over Nazi-occupied Europe. It proved highly successful, functioning to a peak range of 300 miles. Day or night, in any weather, Gee-equipped aircraft could get close to their targets, then find their way back to within a few hundred yards of their home landing strips.

Meanwhile, in the United States, a similar system known as Loran was developed quite independently between 1940 and 1943. Operating at a lower radio frequency than Gee enabled Loran—its name short for Long Range Navigation—to achieve much better coverage, especially over water. During the day, its range was between 700 and 800 nautical miles. At night, this limit was almost doubled, owing to reflection of the skyward-bound portion of the broadcast radio waves from the earth's ionosphere.

Each of these radio navigational systems, the Decca Navigator, Gee, and Loran, represented a huge advance over ordinary celestial position fixing. Fast, and relatively unhindered by poor weather conditions, they were also simple enough for military personnel to learn how to operate quickly. This was important, because the burgeoning Allied forces needed thousands of new navigators for their ships and aircraft.

Under wartime conditions, the U.S. Navy allocated sixteen weeks to train someone in the mathematics, astronomy, and geography required to become a celestial navigator, and this assumed that the student already had the requisite groundwork in those subjects. The rookie navigator would then be able to obtain a celestial fix in clear weather in ten to twenty minutes. By contrast, the same individual could be trained to operate Loran in less than one week and to obtain a fix, comparable in accuracy to that of the celestial method, in less than six minutes.

After the war ended in 1945, the development of Loran and Decca continued

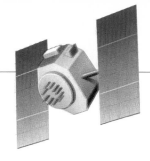

in a peaceful competition that saw the British and American governments and private companies supporting their respective systems. Decca was in commercial use in British coastal waters by 1947, and at the same time chains of Loran stations were established along the coasts of North America. Because of its shorter range, Gee was eventually superseded by the two other systems. Soon aircraft began using the navigation aids as well, and the high-pressure demands of aviation led to rapid advances in navigation technology.

Commercial airliners of the late 1940s moved about ten times as fast as a swift ship, which meant that faulty navigation could get an airplane into trouble much more quickly. As long as every plane carried a qualified navigator who could work out regular Decca or Loran fixes, pilots could count on being well informed; but for economy's sake the airline companies were eager to reduce the size of their flight crews. The ideal solution seemed to be an instrument that would take over the plotting of positions on a chart, providing the pilot with continuous fixes.

The Decca Flight Log, first demonstrated in 1950, quickly found a place in airliner cockpits by providing just such a service. The device incorporated aeronautical charts for the plane's intended route on ten-inch-wide rolls. The rolls crawled across the face of a display unit while a moving pen traced the actual track of the plane onto the paper. Not only could a pilot tell at a glance where he was, he also had a permanent record of the aircraft's course throughout the entire trip.

At the heart of the Flight Log was a computer that translated the output from a standard Decca receiver into positional information; two motors rolled the chart across the ten-by-four-inch viewing area and moved the pen across the chart. But the computer technology of the period was still primitive; a device as big as a room would have been needed to convert the hyperbolic curves of the Decca lattice to precise coordinates on the rectilinear grid of a conventional chart. To meet the size and weight limits imposed on aircraft instruments, Decca's engineers instead used a small, simple machine and plotted the coordinates on special charts that had slight distortions matching the known errors of the computer.

The Decca Flight Log and similar air-navigation devices were in wide use by the end of the 1950s; most ships, however, were still equipped with Decca or Loran receivers that were only slightly more sophisticated than the origi-

nal Blue Gasmeter Jobs. Not until the early 1970s and the advent of inexpensive but very powerful microprocessors did radio navigation once again take a technological leap.

With a microelectronic brain, a "smart" Decca or Loran receiver no longer required a trained navigator to decipher cryptic dial readings and then plot the results by hand onto a chart. Instead, a built-in microprocessor, racing through all the necessary mathematical transformations in a fraction of a second, could flash up the vessel's position directly as latitude and longitude on a continuously updated digital display. Improved plotters, larger and more accurate than the old Flight Log, could automatically trace the craft's course; alternatively, video monitors could show position on electronic maps. The mariner and the aviator thus had at their disposal speedy, precise navigational aids that required neither technical knowledge nor highly specialized training.

The newest versions of these devices can determine the position of a supertanker, for example, with sufficient accuracy that the giant vessel may be steered safely into port through a narrow channel under almost any conditions. But the uses of such navigational gear go beyond wayfinding. For example, the equipment can trace the course plied by a fishing smack, so the crew can avoid going over the same area twice. On the other hand, if one spot proves especially abundant in fish, it can be found again, even in poor visibility and heavy seas. And undersea wrecks—which often make the richest fishing grounds—may be approached closely without the risk that valuable trawling gear will become snagged. In the air, accurate position information may be crucial to the success of a search-and-rescue mission, or for the safe landing of a helicopter on a fogged-in oil platform offshore.

Today, chains of British Decca transmitters cover the coastal waters of northwestern Europe, the North Atlantic, southern Africa, and parts of Asia. The rival American Loran system also serves the North Atlantic, as well as much of North America and strategic stretches of the Pacific. Yet neither system is worldwide and continuous. There are great gaps in coverage, especially over large land-

masses and over much of the Southern Hemisphere, where broad expanses of ocean provide few sites for land-based transmitters. For these areas, radio guidance comes from above.

BEACONS IN THE SKY

On October 4, 1957, the Soviet Union stunned the world with its launch of *Sputnik I,* the first human-made object to be hurled into earth orbit. Even as the persistent "peep-peep" of *Sputnik*'s radio transmitter sounded an alarm to western military thinkers, two American physicists studied the signals with cooler scientific interest. At Baltimore's Johns Hopkins University, William H. Guier and George C. Weiffenbach were intrigued by the rise and fall in frequency of *Sputnik*'s transmissions as the satellite alternately approached and receded from their observing equipment. From the change in frequency, known as a Doppler shift, they were able to work out the satellite's line-of-sight velocity toward or away from the receiver.

Soon the two researchers made a key discovery: By taking regular measurements of *Sputnik*'s velocity every few seconds during the time it was visible and then performing some complex mathematics, they could derive a complete description of the satellite's orbit. A colleague at Johns Hopkins, Frank T. McClure, turned this logic on its head. He demonstrated that, just as the Doppler data gathered at a known location could be used to pinpoint a satellite, if the position of the satellite were known precisely, the Doppler observations could equally well be used to locate the receiving station. That is, a satellite could help provide a navigational fix if its orbit was known.

The ink was barely dry on McClure's seminal paper before the U.S. Government seized upon his theory as the basis for an operational system. Known as Transit, it would become a navigational aid for the military; its initial goal was to supply accurate position fixes for Polaris guided-missile submarines. Eventually made available for commercial use, Transit opened up the nascent field of satellite navigation.

STEERING BY A SYNTHETIC STAR

Transit went to work for the U.S. Navy in January of 1964 and is still in service. Circling in orbits 580 miles high, its five component satellites trace a sort of celestial birdcage within which the earth revolves. From each of the satellites, radio signals of a precisely controlled frequency are beamed down to the earth's surface. Not all of the radio transmission is used for Doppler observations. Sometimes the satellites issue a kind of positional bulletin, vital to the success of the system.

As McClure's theoretical work had shown, to obtain a fix the navigator must know exactly where in time and space a satellite is when it transmits the signals that yield Doppler data. The developers of Transit realized that complex gravitational and atmospheric effects precluded any accurate forecast of a satellite's orbit more than a few days in advance. It would be out of the question, for instance, to list orbital data in a standard nautical almanac that was printed months before it was used. To get the crucial information to the user, practicality dictated that it be transmitted from the satellite itself. But how? It was clear that in this, as in every other aspect of satellite navigation, the answer lay in the creative use of computers.

In the event, each Transit satellite was fitted with a magnetic memory—an erasable storage device with just enough space to hold a listing of the craft's anticipated positions at specific times over a twelve-hour period. Every two minutes, from its memory, the satellite sent out a burst of information—including positional data for the two-minute period following the start of the transmission. On earth, a receiver tuned to the satellite's signal gleaned from it the spacecraft's exact position at that time. Other equipment, linked to the receiver, measured the Doppler shift of the incoming signals. Then all of this information—orbital data plus Doppler data—was shuttled to a small computer. Moments later, its intricate mathematical puzzle solved, the computer responded automatically, giving the receiver's current position as latitude and longitude.

The whole of this ingenious system depends upon the contents of each satellite's memory being regularly updated. To this end, three tracking stations continually monitor the orbital status of all the satellites, passing on their findings to the Transit system's headquarters in Point Mugu, California. There, a battery of large computers toils day and night to divine, based upon the latest observed orbital parameters, the movements of the satellite fleet for the next twelve hours. These new time-and-position figures are then rushed to special "injection stations" in California and Minnesota. They in turn fire off radio messages, causing the satellites to clear their memories and load in the latest batch of navigational data.

When it was made available for civilian use in 1967, Transit was a very expensive system. But the coming of mass-produced microprocessors steadily pushed down costs, and Transit's use spread accordingly. Today, the equipment needed both to receive and to analyze satellite signals may be found even aboard modest sailboats.

Even Transit has its limits. For example, a user might have to wait a long time—up to twelve hours at the equator—for a suitable satellite to come within range. In addition, although Transit may pinpoint a vessel's position accurately to within thirty yards, this is only a surface fix; it is not as useful for aircraft, which are much better served by three-dimensional information that includes altitude. In any case, Transit falls short of the extreme accuracy demanded of certain military

applications, as well as some futuristic modes of transport—for example, as a method of automatically guiding vehicles on land.

PATHFINDER OF TOMORROW

By the 1980s an extraordinary new satellite-based navigational aid was being developed. The Global Positioning System (GPS), also called Navstar, offers position fixes and timing information to users anywhere on the surface of the earth with an accuracy and availability that far surpass those of Transit, Loran, or any other rival.

Each of Navstar's planned twenty-four satellites will move in an orbit 10,900 miles high. They will be arranged so that, for an observer on the earth's surface, at least five of the satellites will always be in view. With appropriate equipment, users will be able to lock onto the signals from three satellites at once and so obtain, by computer, a surface fix accurate perhaps to within thirty feet. Airborne receivers, by gathering data simultaneously from a quartet of satellites, will be able to determine an aircraft's precise altitude—a feature potentially of great importance to commercial airlines.

Similar in principle to Transit, the Navstar satellite positioning system features an array of monitor and injection stations linked to a master control station at Vandenburg Air Force Base in California. Each satellite transmits orbital data and timing signals, the latter supplied from an onboard atomic clock. Like Transit, GPS is intended mainly for military purposes, so that, at the push of a few buttons, the armed forces of the United States and its closest allies will have access to navigational data of unprecedented quality. In addition to yielding extremely accurate position fixes, GPS will enable a vehicle's speed to be determined to the nearest one-tenth of a meter per second and the time of day to within an astonishing thirty-five billionths of a second.

It is almost certain that GPS eventually will be offered for civilian use. But a critical question, still to be decided, is whether the capacity for high accuracy will also be made available, so that the system's full potential can be exploited in automobiles, ships, and planes. If this is the case, then the possibilities for GPS are almost limitless.

In civil aviation, GPS might permit more planes to pass safely through already crowded airspace. At present, transatlantic flights, for example, must be separated vertically by about one third of a mile; halving this safety margin could double the number of aircraft flying at altitudes where fuel consumption is most efficient. More precise navigation would also make direct routing simpler and perhaps ease the congestion at busy airports.

On the ground, emergency services would benefit. At fire, police, ambulance, or Coast Guard headquarters, a controller might feed the GPS-supplied coordinates of a reported disaster directly into a vehicle's computer, so that an emergency team could simply follow its directions to get where it was needed. Adding a transmitter that could report to a central office the position worked out by the GPS receiver would help authorities track the whereabouts of rescue machinery and personnel. A similar system would allow the close monitoring of cargoes of hazardous waste, or it could automatically report the location of police and security guards on night duty. As receivers eventually become as small as a cigar box and cost only a few hundred dollars, virtually anyone from a space shuttle pilot to a wilderness hiker could become a regular user.

THE NAVIGATOR WITHIN

In addition to radio navigation, a radically different method of position finding progressed rapidly during World War II. Called inertial navigation, it was essentially an application of twentieth-century technology to the ancient art of dead reckoning *(pages 57-65)*. Instead of relying on signals from outside sources, this new method made use of inertia, the propensity of all matter to resist change in its state of motion.

Simple in concept, inertial navigation requires first that a vehicle's whereabouts be recorded at the start of its journey. Then, during transit, all of the accelerations and decelerations the craft undergoes are measured. From these, the speeds and distances traveled are derived by a mathematical maneuver called integration. Finally, the total calculated displacement is tacked onto the original known position to yield a navigational fix.

While straightforward in principle, the realization of inertial systems as a precise navigational aid came only after decades of applied ingenuity. One of the key elements needed to create such a system was a fixed frame of reference, within the vehicle, against which to gauge its acceleration. A device able to provide this was well known a century ago. It was the gyroscope, a ring-mounted rotating wheel that will keep its original plane no matter which way the ring is turned. As early as 1914, the device had formed the basis of an automatic pilot for holding an airplane in straight and level flight.

As part of an inertial navigation system, the gyroscope assumed a different role. It would stabilize a perfectly level, independent platform, relative to which the degree and direction of any changes in speed could be judged. In order to measure these changes, or accelerations, a second instrument was needed—an accelerometer *(page 58)*.

The essential part of the accelerometer is a pendulum. When there is no change in motion, the pendulum hangs straight down in the null position. If the craft alters speed, the pendulum, because of its inertia—its reluctance to move— is swung off that position. From the amount of swing, the acceleration at each moment can be determined; these continuous measurements in turn are used to

work out the distance traveled in a given time in a given direction. This last step involves a third crucial component: The integrator sums up the measured accelerations to produce a calculated displacement.

Not until July 1942 was the first practical inertial system put into action. Perched atop a German V-2 rocket missile, it sat only a few feet from the deadly warhead in the missile's nose cone. It was in fact more of an autopilot—a steering mechanism—than an aid to position finding. Its twin gyroscopes, used to stabilize the rocket in flight, cooperated with a single accelerometer working along the direction of thrust. The accelerometer incorporated a mechanical integrator, which essentially counted the revolutions of an electric motor turning at a rate proportional to the acceleration. When the total indicated that the missile had reached its target velocity, a signal was sent to shut off the engines. For the first time, even though it fell short of performing as a navigational aid, the triad of gyroscope, accelerometer, and integrator had been brought together as a team.

By the 1950s, the harnessing of the atom had led to the development of the nuclear-powered submarine, which could remain submerged for long periods, evading scrutiny by potential adversaries. But this capacity would be seriously compromised if the submarine periodically had to be brought up to periscope (or antenna) depth to fix its position by the stars or by radio beacon.

Inertial navigation offered the ideal solution to such a problem. After a decade of postwar development work in the United States, this self-contained method of pathfinding had matured to the stage where it could be used reliably aboard surface vessels at sea. And a nuclear sub could use it to steer accurately even while it remained invisible far beneath the waves—a fact dramatically demonstrated in 1958 when the USS *Nautilus* achieved the world's first under-the-ice voyage across the North Pole.

TAKEOFF FOR INERTIAL NAVIGATION

Contributing greatly to the growing importance of inertial systems were electronic computers. During the 1950s computers gradually took over from mechanical integrators (such as those used on the V-2 and *Nautilus)* the final task of processing the data gathered by accelerometers.

In practice, a pair of accelerometers, set at right angles to each other, was needed to measure changes in a vessel's speed in both the north-south and east-west directions. Each of their measurements subsequently had to be integrated twice: first to yield the cumulative speed, then the displacement. Not only could a computer far outpace any set of mechanical devices in carrying out these integrations, it also was much more accurate; it was unaffected by such factors as temperature changes or internal friction, which could cause unpredictable errors in a mechanical system.

At first, the only computers available to mate with inertial systems were of the analog type. Relatively small and simple, they were basically electronic versions of the mechanical integrators and could deal directly with the continuously varying electrical signals sent out by the accelerometers. Their weakness, however, was a lack of precision. Digital computers, on the other hand, were initially too large and heavy. Only as their components shrank in size were these more-powerful machines able to supplant their analog cousins.

Civilian airlines followed the emergence of computerized inertial navigation with keen interest. In crowded airways such as those over the North Atlantic, more-accurate course keeping could allow a reduction in the required separation between planes, so that more traffic could use the same airspace. With fuel costs comprising an increasing part of the airlines' operating expenses, minutes of flight time saved by precise navigation would be a welcome economy.

By the late 1960s, two manufacturers, Litton Industries and General Motors, had introduced inertial systems for commercial use. Both were marvels of microengineering, tailored to the cramped environs of an aircraft cockpit. Litton's LTN-51 model, for example, weighed only sixty-five pounds, complete with a power supply and miniature computer built from integrated circuits. In 1968, Boeing began to fit computerized inertial systems aboard its new 747 Jumbo Jets, and in 1970, Pan American used the system for the first time on a commercial flight.

Today, inertial navigation is common on all long-range jets. Typically, three separate, identical systems (one in use and two for backup) are installed in the cockpit. Before takeoff, one of the flight crew uses a digital keyboard on each unit to enter the latitude and longitude of the flight's starting point, as well as a series of way points along the planned route. Once aloft, the navigation system can be connected to the autopilot so that the plane stays on course, with correctional turns automatically executed at each of the way points.

So precise and reliable are these inertial systems that they make transoceanic flying a mundane trade, thus giving rise to a novel problem. Pilots tend to trust their mechanical navigators so much that they sometimes neglect to double-check their position by other methods during a flight. Many experts believe that such complacency was behind the navigational failure that led to a Korean Airlines 747 being shot down over the Soviet Union in 1983 with the loss of all 269 people on board. The plane was 350 miles off course—an error that could have been caused by a single wrong digit in the initial position keyed into the primary inertial navigation system before the plane took off.

MOVING MAPS FOR THE MOTORIST

Although travelers on the oceans and in the air have reaped tremendous benefits from electronic and computer-based navigation, little of this technology has yet trickled down to the most populous of wayfarers, the motorist, who still must rely upon traditional signposts, personal knowledge, and the folding map. But that too, may be changing.

In 1984, a small engineering company named Etak, Incorporated, in Menlo Park, California, announced what it claimed was the first practical automatic navigation system for cars and trucks. One of Etak's founders, Stan Honey, had previously designed a customized position-fixing device, using Loran, that helped a yacht win two transpacific races from Los Angeles to Honolulu. It was during one of those long voyages that Honey's thoughts first turned to a pathfinding system that might work inside an ordinary automobile. For this, Honey later realized, any method based upon incoming radio signals, such as Loran, was impractical, since in urban areas the signals would tend to be blocked or distorted.

Instead, Honey developed a system that relies on dead reckoning; that is, it works out a vehicle's current position from a known starting point. Sensors located near the car's wheels count their turns to tell how far the car has traveled, while an electronic compass placed in the roof or rear window determines the direction of travel. A computer, with the processing power of a typical home personal computer, mounted in the trunk, correlates this information with an electronic map. The map is stored on a tape cassette, along with an index of street addresses and intersections.

When in use, the map is displayed on a four-and-one-half-inch-wide video screen, supported on a flexible stalk in front of the dashboard. At the center of the screen is a small triangle, depicting the car. The driver enters the starting position into the system, using a small keypad to search the index and select the correct location. When the automobile moves, the triangle remains stationary at the center of the screen while the labeled features of the map—streets, highways, and other landmarks—move around it; whatever streets face the driver through the windshield are also ahead of the vehicle on the screen. If the driver makes a turn, the map reorients itself so that it continues to correspond with the view outside.

The moving map was another inspiration rooted in Honey's interest in sailing. From studies of navigation history he recalled that for centuries primitive Polynesians have been able to steer confidently across vast distances of the Pacific Ocean without the aid of instruments. Instead of plotting their course across a map, they imagine their canoes to be stationary while, all around them, the world glides past. It is this "movement" of islands that the Polynesian navigators study and remember. They call their method *etak,* and Honey decided to borrow the name as well as the concept for his system of automotive navigation.

The landlocked version of Etak has met with some commercial success: General Motors bought a 30 percent interest in the company, with an eye to offering the system as an option in its higher-priced cars. Perhaps more important, however, is the standard set by Etak's ingenious use of computers to maintain the accuracy of the system despite the twists, turns, and bumps of the road. No other inexpensive system had been able to keep tiny errors in measurement from building up into gross inaccuracies. Etak avoids this by using comparisons with the electronic maps to recalibrate the sensors and to correct the accumulated error. Once every second, the computer in the Etak Navigator compares distance and direction measurements to features on the map. If the car has driven around a particular S-bend, and the map shows a road with an identical S-bend a short distance from the car's indicated position, the Etak computer decides that the vehicle actually is on that section of road. This constant correction allows the Navigator to remain consistently accurate to within about fifty feet.

TOWARD THE CREWLESS SHIP

One of the principal elements of the Etak system, the electronic chart, also has begun to find a place in ocean navigation. Ships can carry a complete set of such charts, stored on magnetic or optical disks. Requiring much less space than their paper counterparts while supplying as much information, digital charts are also easier to update; corrected versions can be stored electronically at a fraction of the cost in time and money required to replace paper charts. But their real advantage is in the way that electronic charts can be manipulated by a computer.

When displayed on a video terminal, a chart can be combined with current data from radar and navigational systems, so the captain can see at a glance exactly where his ship is, and what other ships nearby are doing. Longer-term planning of a voyage can be conducted by plotting a number of prospective routes on the terminal; the computer, referring to tables of currents, tides, and prevailing winds, can help determine the optimum course to the ship's destination.

A central computer programmed for navigation as well as for controlling the ship can do still more. Informed by navigation systems about the vessel's position, and by the captain about where the vessel is to go, the computer can take the helm. By comparing the programmed route with up-to-the-minute navigational data from radio or inertial systems, the computer can make precise adjustments to the rudder angle and engine speed to keep the vessel on course and schedule. If radar is included in the computer loop, the ship can even act automatically to avoid a collision. If the radar data warns that some obstacle, such as another vessel, is dangerously close, the main computer can immediately alert the ship's autopilot to manipulate engine and rudder controls for evasive action.

It is becoming clear that such integrated systems can revolutionize the nature of sea and air travel. The extent to which it has already done so was vividly illustrated on January 15, 1984, when the Dutch freighter *Pergo* went aground north of Dunbar, Scotland. Local coast guards were astounded to discover that the ship, her lights ablaze and engines running, had crossed 200 miles of the North Sea from the coast of Norway without a soul on board. Battered by a ferocious storm, the *Pergo*'s five-man crew had feared that she was on the verge of foundering and had abandoned the vessel two days earlier. The computer-equipped *Pergo* had subsequently steered herself, with uncanny precision, across one of the world's roughest stretches of water to within a few miles of her intended destination. Ships without crews may never become the norm, but the *Pergo*'s hands-off voyage showed that, with computers at the helm, even that is not impossible.

New Tools for the Navigator

Until recently, the sextant and chronometer were the chief wayfinding tools of mariners traveling across the featureless landscape of the ocean. Latitude and longitude were determined by observing the angle of the sun or stars above the horizon, noting the precise time of the sightings, and consulting tables that link this data to positional information. But celestial navigation, as this procedure is called, requires considerable training. The navigator must make a complex series of calculations, and even a small error in measuring the angle of a celestial body can place a vessel many miles away from its actual position. Even more of an art—and less exact—is navigation by dead reckoning, a technique that involves using a ship's compass heading and estimated speed (with allowance for the effect of wind and currents) to keep track of a ship's whereabouts.

As explained on the following pages, today's voyagers have at hand a number of computerized navigational aids that yield more accurate results with no need for human calculations. One system, called inertial navigation, employs sensitive instruments that detect the slightest changes in course and speed to give dead reckoning an unprecedented degree of precision. Radio-navigation systems, in which computers determine a ship's position based on the time it takes a radio signal to arrive from ground- or satellite-based transmitters, have largely supplanted the chronometer and sextant. Even charts, perhaps the most basic of the navigator's tools, have been translated into electronic form. With such a system, the navigator can elect not to plot a course; the computer does it automatically.

Inertial Navigation

Navigation by dead reckoning has always been notoriously inaccurate because a ship is rarely traveling at the speed or in the direction it seems to be. Currents and winds can slow a vessel, speed it up, or push it off course in ways that are too subtle to perceive.

But an inertial-navigation system can perform dead reckoning with astonishing exactitude. All it needs is a starting point with a known location (a pier or a buoy, for example) and detailed information on the ship's acceleration—that is, any change in its speed or direction. Because acceleration measures the combined effect of all the forces acting on a vessel—thrust from engine or sail, the push of tidal currents, and wind on the hull—it is the only factor that the system must attend to. Small errors accumulate, but maritime inertial-navigation computers are programmed to consult other position-finding systems *(pages 60-63)* to correct them.

At the heart of the technique is a device called an inertial-measurement unit. Also known as an IMU, it consists of a platform, stabilized by gyroscopes, that is isolated from the pitch, roll, and yaw of the ship by a three-axis framework called gimbals. Mounted on the platform is a pair of accelerometers, which use a combination of electrical-current flow and magnetism *(below)* to measure acceleration north or south, and east or west *(below)*.

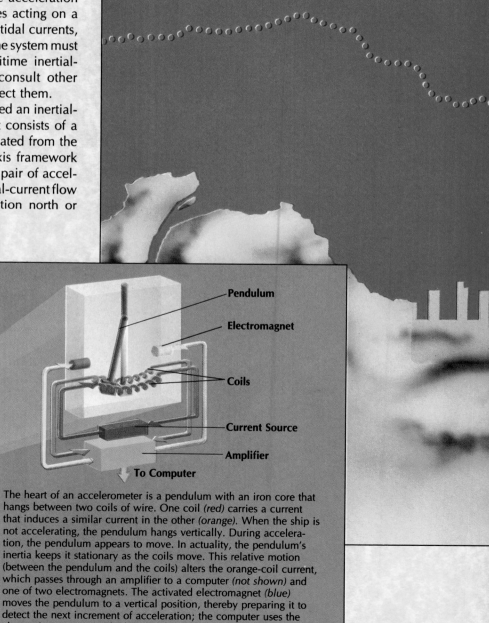

A Stable Platform for Sensing Acceleration

Pendulum

Electromagnet

Coils

Current Source

Amplifier

To Computer

Accelerometer

Gyroscope

The heart of an accelerometer is a pendulum with an iron core that hangs between two coils of wire. One coil *(red)* carries a current that induces a similar current in the other *(orange)*. When the ship is not accelerating, the pendulum hangs vertically. During acceleration, the pendulum appears to move. In actuality, the pendulum's inertia keeps it stationary as the coils move. This relative motion (between the pendulum and the coils) alters the orange-coil current, which passes through an amplifier to a computer *(not shown)* and one of two electromagnets. The activated electromagnet *(blue)* moves the pendulum to a vertical position, thereby preparing it to detect the next increment of acceleration; the computer uses the change in current to calculate acceleration.

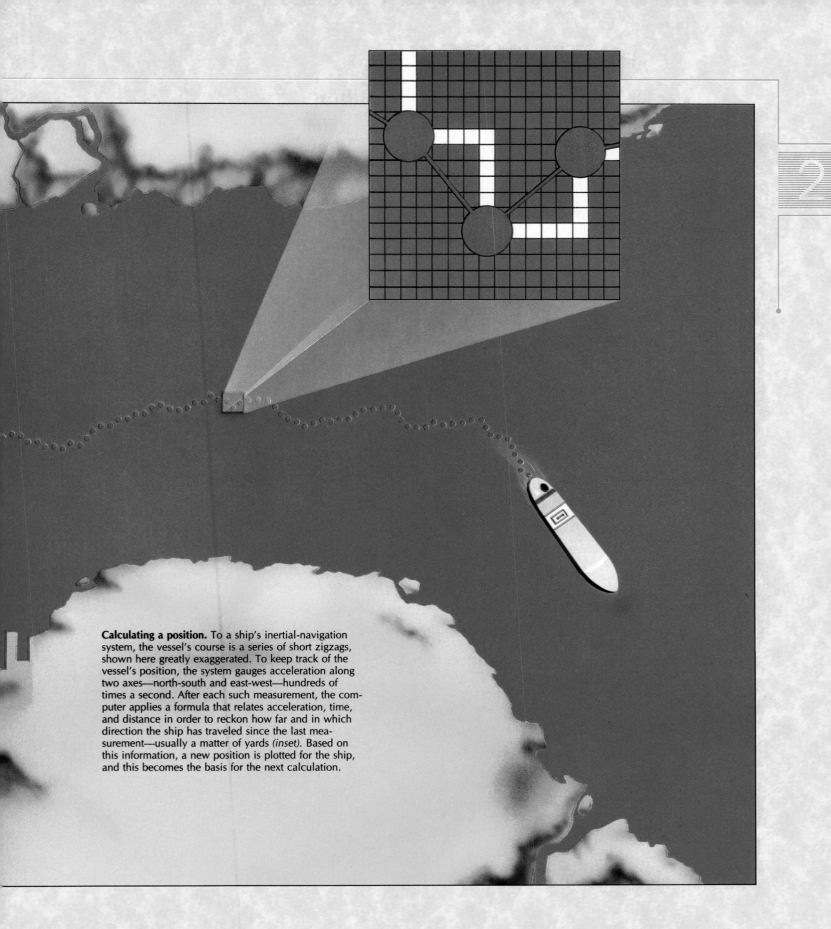

Calculating a position. To a ship's inertial-navigation system, the vessel's course is a series of short zigzags, shown here greatly exaggerated. To keep track of the vessel's position, the system gauges acceleration along two axes—north-south and east-west—hundreds of times a second. After each such measurement, the computer applies a formula that relates acceleration, time, and distance in order to reckon how far and in which direction the ship has traveled since the last measurement—usually a matter of yards *(inset)*. Based on this information, a new position is plotted for the ship, and this becomes the basis for the next calculation.

Curves of Time and Position

More common than inertial navigation systems aboard ships is Loran (Long Range Navigation). This method of position finding uses groups of shore-based radio transmitters—a master and no fewer than two secondary stations—to send synchronized radio signals to shipboard receivers. As many as twenty times a second, the master transmitter sends out a radio signal. After receiving the transmission, each secondary station transmits a signal.

A Loran receiver intercepts all the signals. They are timed so that no matter where a ship may be within the range of the transmitters, the master signal always arrives first, followed by the secondary transmissions in a predetermined order. A timer in the receiver starts counting tenths of microseconds when it detects the master signal. As explained on these pages, the intervals between the arrival of the master signal and two secondary signals are used to determine the ship's position.

The computer's chief contributions to Loran are accuracy and convenience. To obtain a Loran fix without a computer built into a receiver, the navigator had to adjust the set by hand to determine the delay between master and secondary signals. A computer can perform this task much more quickly and precisely. Furthermore, a computer can display interval measurements directly as latitude and longitude. And by using successive position calculations, the computer provides an up-to-the-minute report of the ship's progress.

Lines of Position

In Loran, a master station and a secondary station transmit radio signals that together define a family of imaginary lines called lines of position. Each line consists of points on the earth where the interval between the arrival of the two signals, adjusted for the lag of the secondary signals behind the master signals, is the same. Five such lines are shown here, but in actuality, there are an infinite number of them—all curves called hyperbolas. Where the two signals arrive simultaneously (after built-in delays have been accounted for), the hyperbola happens to be a straight line, midway between the two stations.

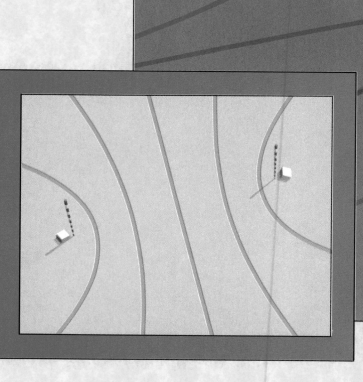

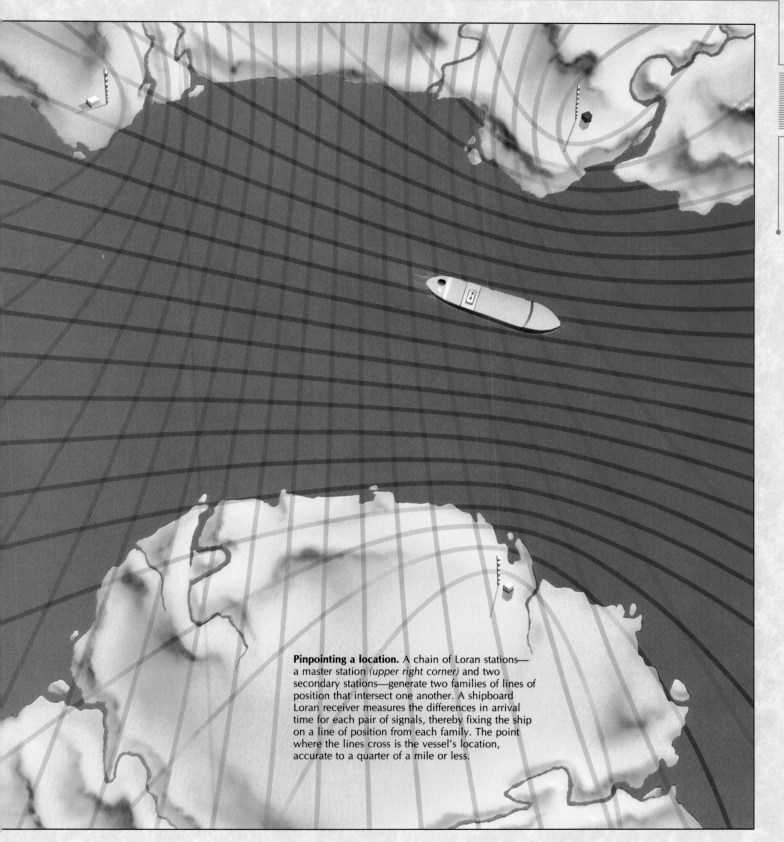

Pinpointing a location. A chain of Loran stations—a master station *(upper right corner)* and two secondary stations—generate two families of lines of position that intersect one another. A shipboard Loran receiver measures the differences in arrival time for each pair of signals, thereby fixing the ship on a line of position from each family. The point where the lines cross is the vessel's location, accurate to a quarter of a mile or less.

Navigating by Satellite

A radio-navigation system even more accurate than Loran is based on an array of satellites in low-earth orbit. Called the Global Positioning System (GPS), or Navstar, the 24-satellite network is scheduled for completion in the 1990s. With Navstar, a shipboard receiver calculates the distance between the vessel and three of the two dozen satellites. As shown here, these distances—together with the locations of the three satellites—are sufficient to fix the ship's location. When fully operational, Navstar is expected to provide positions potentially accurate to ten yards, anywhere on the globe.

Though simple in concept, pinpointing a satellite and measuring the distance between it and a ship present a challenge. Not only are the ship and receiver in motion, but so are the transmitters, whizzing around the globe at thousands of miles an hour. Furthermore, these measurements must be extraordinarily precise if they are to yield accurate fixes.

To provide this precision, a computer in each Navstar satellite is programmed to generate a unique, seven-day-long sequence of ones and zeros called the P-code. Transmitting at the rate of more than ten million bits per second, the satellite continually recycles this code, beginning each Saturday at midnight Greenwich time. A computer in the Navstar receiver is also programmed to generate the P-code at the same rate and according to the same schedule.

Upon the arrival of a segment of P-code from a satellite, a clock inside a Navstar receiver notes the time. Then the receiver compares the sequence of ones and zeros from the satellite to the P-code its own computer has generated to determine when the satellite transmitted the P-code segment. The difference between the two times—a matter of microseconds—is a measure of the distance between ship and satellite.

The missing element for determining the ship's position is the location of the satellite at the instant in question. To enable the computer in the receiver to calculate this crucial fact, ground stations monitor the changes in satellite orbits caused by aerodynamic drag in the thin atmosphere scores of miles above the earth; the ground stations also detect clock errors aboard the satellites that may cause the P-code to be transmitted as much as several hundred microseconds off schedule. Correction factors are radioed to the satellites, which relay them to any Navstar receiver tuned in to the system.

A circle of possibilities. To compute the distance to a satellite, the computer in a Navstar receiver aboard a ship multiplies the time a radio signal takes to arrive from the satellite by the signal's velocity, the speed of light. Having calculated the distance to the satellite and knowing its position, the computer can determine that the ship lies somewhere on a circle (*above*), every point of which is the same distance from the satellite.

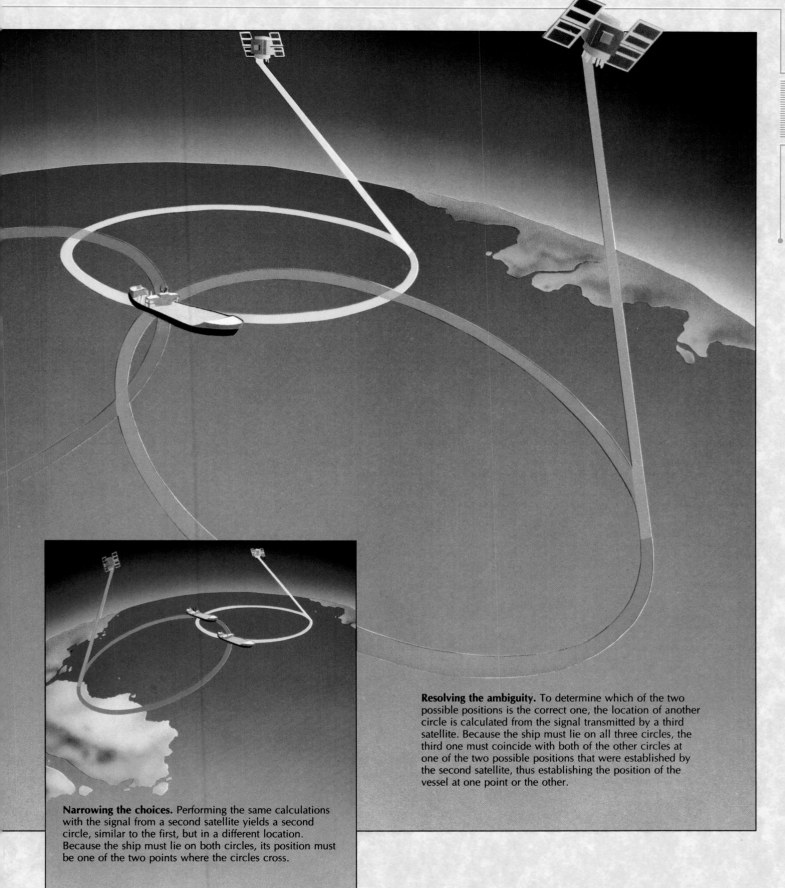

2

Resolving the ambiguity. To determine which of the two possible positions is the correct one, the location of another circle is calculated from the signal transmitted by a third satellite. Because the ship must lie on all three circles, the third one must coincide with both of the other circles at one of the two possible positions that were established by the second satellite, thus establishing the position of the vessel at one point or the other.

Narrowing the choices. Performing the same calculations with the signal from a second satellite yields a second circle, similar to the first, but in a different location. Because the ship must lie on both circles, its position must be one of the two points where the circles cross.

63

Electronic Charts

Nautical charts are crammed with vital information: descriptions of coastlines and channels; positions of buoys and beacons; distances, water depths, and more. But the printed chart deals with a fixed world, independent of such transitory facts as a ship's position, its heading, or the movements of other vessels nearby.

In new electronic-chart systems now coming into use, the fixed and the transitory are melded. At the heart of such a system is a desktop-size computer that processes navigational information stored on magnetic or optical disks. The computer is linked to a ship's Loran or Navstar receiver (pages 60-63), which provides the ship's latitude and longitude. From that information, a computerized chart system chooses a section of the chart for display on a monitor, and the navigator can zoom in for a close-up look. The ship's position appears on the chart, along with its heading (the computer is also linked to a compass). Successive Loran or Navstar fixes enable the computer to calculate the ship's speed by noting the distance traveled in a given time.

Radar echoes of watercraft and buoys are displayed in red for strong echoes (usually from large objects) or magenta for weaker ones. Water is shown in shades of blue, the darker hue reserved for shoals. Except for prominent landmarks that are used as navigation aids, such as radio-transmitter antennae, radar blips from objects on land are suppressed in order to give a clearer picture of the waterborne obstacles that a ship might confront.

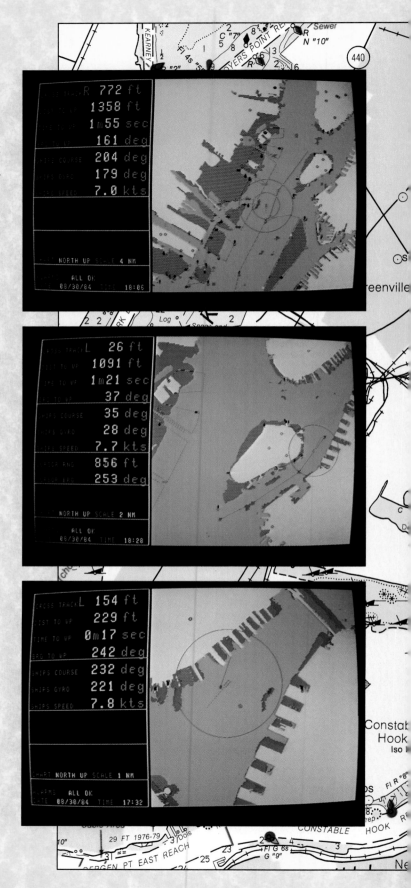

Navigating by electronic chart. Three computerized views of New York Harbor show areas ranging from sixteen square nautical miles (top) to one square nautical mile (bottom). In each case, the ship is represented by a rectangle. Circles encompass objects within a quarter mile and a half mile of the ship. A black dashed line from the bow of the ship indicates the vessel's course and where it will be one minute hence. Red dashed lines stand for the vessel's intended course. Waypoints—places where a course change is necessary—appear as red starbursts. Buoys are displayed as black symbols, which are overlaid with red or magenta if they appear on radar. Numbers on the screen's left are, from the top: distance off course; distance, time, and direction to the next waypoint; the ship's desired course; its heading; and its speed in knots.

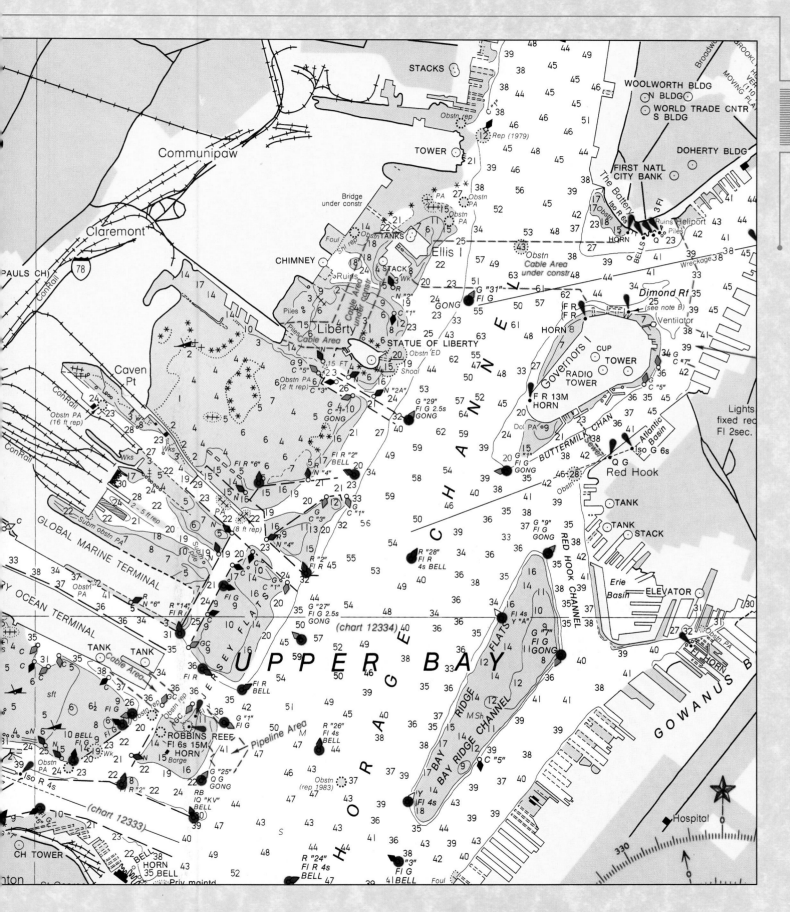

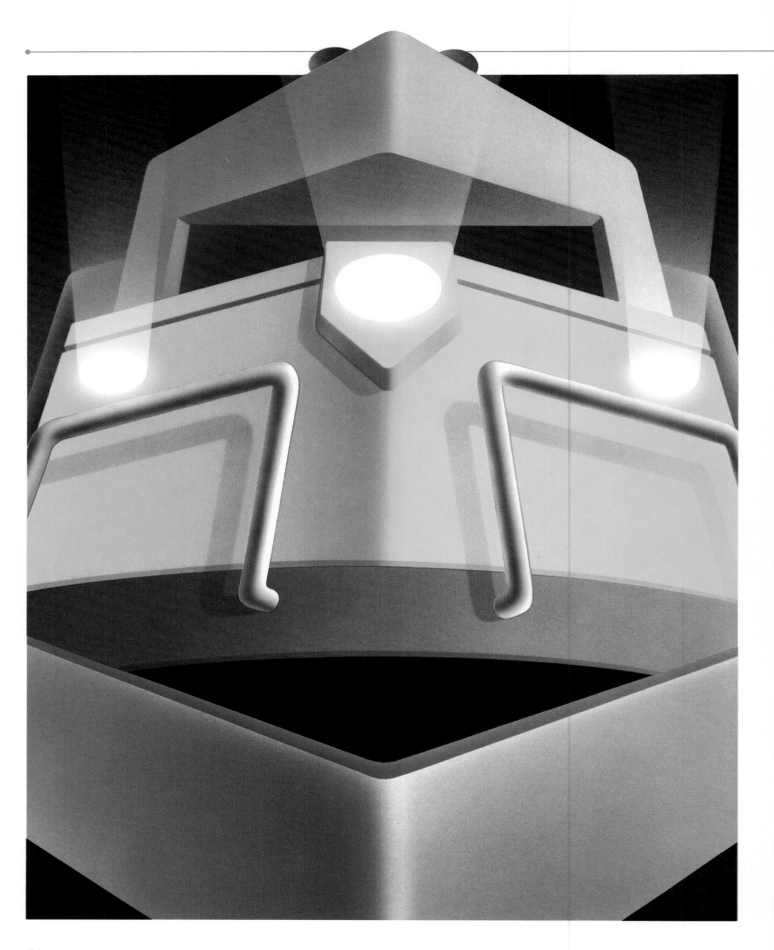

Of Origins and Destinations

3

Every day, more than a billion tons of imported goods arrive from all over the world at some three hundred ports of entry into the United States. At each terminal, U.S. Customs Service inspectors collect tariffs, ferret out illegal drugs and other contraband, and police import quotas. The inspectors are also responsible for enforcing the rules and regulations of forty other federal agencies that have jurisdiction over various aspects of trade between the United States and other nations. In addition, the Customs Service must prepare statistical reports for a number of government agencies, such as the Internal Revenue Service, the Bureau of the Census, the Treasury Department, and the Immigration and Naturalization Service.

Once through Customs, everything from Irish linen to Japanese-made stereos and Kenyan coffee wends its way to destinations across North America by train, truck, and aircraft, all linked together in a vast, interconnected distribution system. The complexity of the enterprise is staggering. Even the transportation of domestic goods within the United States—shipping grapes from California to Maine, for instance, or automobiles from Detroit to Texas—is rife with the potential for lost or delayed shipments and for other inefficiencies that could cost merchants and shippers millions of dollars a year.

Increasingly, many aspects of freight distribution are being turned over to computers. For instance, the airline industry uses the machines to keep close count of the weight of passengers on every flight. Doing so makes it possible to calculate more easily and accurately how much freight the aircraft can haul. Other carriers, railroads in particular, use computers not only to track the flow of goods from point of origin to destination but to choreograph the entire distribution process.

SAVED FROM DROWNING

More significantly, computers have vanquished—or at least greatly reduced—the oceans of paper that were once needed to keep track of goods from the beginning of their journey to the end, and nowhere is this victory more appreciated than at the U.S. Customs Service. Until relatively recently, the Customs Service performed its manifold tasks largely without the aid of computers. In 1980, for example, the agency relied on paper-based cargo-tracking methods to process nearly four and a half million shipments of foreign goods, arriving mostly by sea. Because of the number of individual shipments arriving on a single vessel and the quantity of paperwork associated with each shipment, an understaffed Customs Service often left freight awaiting inspection for days on piers or in warehouses.

At ports of entry, the flow of paper began even before a ship reached the dock. On shore, customs brokers—individuals or firms licensed by the Customs Service to act as agents for importers—submitted a number of forms for review by customs officials. Similar forms were submitted by the carriers bringing in the

cargo. Customs inspectors and import specialists reviewed the forms as they came in, sometimes returning them to brokers for corrections or additional information. Once all the paperwork was in order, clerical staff could begin keypunching data into the agency's fragmented computer system. Much of this information was then passed on in paper form to various other federal agencies where the data would be keypunched for a second time.

Nowhere were the deficiencies of the agency's antiquated methods more glaring than at the nation's major seaports. Typically, an arriving vessel might carry freight packed into more than twenty-seven hundred stackable twenty-foot-long containers—enough cargo to fill 1,350 railroad cars. As the requisite paperwork made its way through the system, customs trade specialists—using calculators—would assess duties and taxes. Meanwhile, Customs Service inspectors would begin examining shipments. By law, inspectors were supposed to search each shipload in its entirety, spot-checking the contents of most containers and closely scrutinizing the rest. But the realities of staff and time constraints simply did not allow for such a comprehensive examination. As one customs official put it, "What are you going to do, unload every container? We'd have stuff stacked up forever."

Instead, inspectors tried to economize their activities, using instinct, experience, and advice from colleagues about which containers to search closely and which to examine only cursorily. But without a fast, efficient way to share information among Customs Service offices in different parts of the country—to alert agents to suspicious activities, for example—inspectors had to exchange experiences and search strategies by wire. Not surprisingly, the system was slow and porous, and the effectiveness of customs inspection varied considerably from port to port.

The situation cried out for improvement. In 1969, a management consulting firm hired to look into the matter had advised the Customs Service to develop an on-line computer system for the purpose of exchanging information within the agency. The advice went unheeded for several years, in part because Congress and the agency had difficulty reaching a consensus on exactly what was needed. As it happened, when the Customs Service finally acted on the consulting firm's recommendation, it made a flawed decision. In setting out to make up for lost time, the agency attempted to computerize every aspect of its operations simultaneously, rather than tackle the problem one piece at a time and build modules of hardware and software that could later be integrated into a single system.

Top management at Customs created an Office of Automatic Data Processing and staffed it with about two hundred people, most of them lured from the private sector. Not surprisingly, perhaps, many longtime Customs Service managers resisted the sudden push to computerization, and with so many people involved, it was difficult to reach agreement on anything. As Dick Bonner, one of the program analysts who joined the agency during this period, remembered much later, "The thing fell from its own weight."

Eventually the group was reorganized under a new manager, who decided to take the modular approach. By the mid-1970s, the first module was up and running—an automated data-collection system that allowed Customs to enter into its data base a greater amount of detail about each shipment than had previously been recorded. Known as the Early Implementation System, or EIS, this stage of the agency's computerization effort suffered from a major shortcoming: No one had thought to examine whether, and to what degree, customs brokers—who file 95 percent of all the entry documentation handled by customs officials—used computers in their own work. Thus, despite the automation of data collection within the agency, information originating outside still had to be entered into the agency's system by keypunchers. During a period of tight federal budgets, when Congress and the president were telling the Customs Service to trim its staff, the agency was asking for money to hire more keypunchers for a computer system that had originally been presented as a cost-cutting investment. The agency's request for additional funds was denied. In the late 1970s, the Early Implementation System was shut down, and the Customs Service found itself back at square one.

Computers did not go away, however. By 1980, the agency was using them for several tasks, such as tracking duty collections and certifying whether brokers were bonded, a form of insurance that protects the Customs Service against the loss of duties and taxes to dishonest brokers or their employees. But instead of being integrated, the systems were virtually independent of one another, handicapping agency staff members, who often needed information from several sources. Staffers either had to master the software and idiosyncrasies of each system or, more often, seek the help of colleagues who specialized in one system or another. Both methods were less than satisfactory.

Finally, in the early years of the new decade, the Customs Service again took up the quest for a comprehensive computer system. This time, in an effort to make an accurate assessment of its computer needs, the agency conducted a nationwide survey of customs brokers. The study revealed that, of the 900 broker firms questioned, only 175 prepared customs documents on computers. But this automated minority accounted for 60 percent of all entries. In other words, more than half of the data the agency was keypunching into its computers could easily be transferred electronically from brokers' offices.

Galvanized by this rather belated insight, the agency formed a committee, made up of Customs Service data-processing specialists and members of the National Customs Brokers and Forwarders Association of America, to design an electronically linked system for exchanging information. The most complicated

part of the committee's task was agreeing on a message format—essentially, a common language—that all brokers, importers, and others would use when communicating with computers at the Customs Service.

A standard format bridges the communications gap between incompatible computers—machines that employ different operating codes and data transmission rates—by assuring uniform procedures for preparing and transmitting electronic documents. Brokers need not drastically change their existing methods of processing documents for their own internal consumption. Instead, add-on hardware and software, configured to use the common language, can translate information for transmission from a broker's computer and interpret messages sent by the Customs Service. Small-volume brokers who were not prepared to make the electronic linkup themselves could elect to use a data-processing service bureau, an intermediary specializing in the translation of incoming and outgoing electronic messages.

By 1981, the Automated Broker Interface, as the format was named, had undergone successful testing with brokers at the ports of Philadelphia and Baltimore. Further testing followed in New Orleans, Buffalo, and Houston. In April 1984, the Customs Service opened the system—now known as the Automated Commercial System, or ACS—to all businesses nationwide licensed to prepare entries of imported merchandise. Refined and expanded from the original ABI module, the ACS included not only the ABI but other automated components, tailored to keep track of various documents associated with imports, such as collections, bills, enforcement information, bond transfers, and carrier freight lists, or manifests.

As then-commissioner William von Raab noted, the 200-year-old Customs Service had finally and fully entered the Information Age. By 1990, the agency's six central computers—five IBM 3090 600 S machines and an IBM 3090 200 to handle their communications, all located in Washington, D.C.—were handling more than 300 million queries a day from customs brokers, inspectors, carriers, and other interested parties.

A SYSTEM MUCH STREAMLINED
With the ACS, Customs clearance procedures can begin while a cargo ship is still at sea or a plane is still in the air. Each broker responsible for cargo aboard

the incoming vessel prepares entry documents that contain information about the shipment, such as a preliminary listing of the contents, its country of origin, and the U.S. purchasers. The broker transmits the electronic entry directly to the Customs Service's central computers, where the information becomes available to all Customs personnel, including specialists on the scene.

As in precomputer days, if the specialists find errors in the entry documentation or require additional information, they return the document to the broker. But with computers, transmission is electronic, by way of the Customs Service data-processing center in Washington, D.C. The broker keys in the necessary details and electronically fires the document back to the Customs Service for approval. To check on the progress of an entry document, a customs broker merely transmits an inquiry to the ACS computers, which provide a report of the processing status.

Even as these preparations are made on land for the arrival of a cargo-bearing ship or plane, the vessel's crew can use a feature of the ACS called the Automated Manifest System to transmit the manifest—the list of goods aboard—to the Customs Service. Manifests are sent by way of satellite, either directly to the agency or through an intermediary, such as a data-processing service bureau or a port authority. The Automated Manifest System allows customs inspectors to check the actual cargo aboard the ship against the entry documents filed by various brokers and to begin developing a strategy for examining the goods when they arrive at the port.

With broker information and the ship's manifest in hand, specialists can use a module of the ACS known as the Cargo Selectivity System to assess the likelihood of finding contraband or goods that violate a myriad of federal regulations. Within the Cargo Selectivity System, specialists can consult national and local data-base files for results of past examinations of cargo transported by a particular carrier or originating from a specific country. This automated assessment procedure may draw an inspector's attention to certain suspicious items that might otherwise be overlooked. Carriers, whose livelihood depends on being able to maintain a regular schedule, also benefit from the expedited inspection system; the efficient processing of cargo assures the carriers of a quicker return to service.

Once a carrier has arrived and customs inspectors have examined its various

shipments of cargo, several other automated processes kick in before merchandise can be released for distribution. The results of the inspection are entered into the Customs Service data base.

One of the factors that helps determine the duty charged on merchandise, for example, is whether or not the material falls within prescribed quota limits. In some cases, reduced duty rates apply to specified quantities of goods that are entering the United States from favored countries during limited time periods. The ACS Quota Module monitors the quota levels of imported goods and, among other things, feeds this information into a weekly "Quota Critical List," an electronic report that serves to alert brokers and others to the current quota information. Quota processing for electronic entries continues automatically twenty-four hours a day.

From data in the entry summary, the ACS calculates the duties, taxes, and fees owed by the importer or the broker responsible for each shipment and assesses any penalties incurred for such transgressions as tardiness in filing documents or paying duties. In total, these payments to Customs amount to some twenty billion dollars annually. The ACS Financial System tallies the final total due on each shipment (there could be hundreds of shipments on a given vessel), records it in a document called the Entry Summary, and prepares a tariff bill for the appropriate broker. Before the advent of the ACS, brokers paid each bill separately, a record-keeping nightmare that generated paperwork at both ends of the transaction. With the ACS Financial System in place, a broker can request daily a composite statement, payable with a single check, that combines duties and taxes on all the day's shipments. Most brokers pay the bill through an automatic electronic transfer of funds.

Before a shipment is finally released for distribution and its Entry Summary filed in the agency's archives, the Customs Service has a few more details to attend to. For example, the Summary Selectivity System, another segment of the ACS, may flag one of these digests for detailed review by a team of commodity specialists, an automated decision based on criteria similar to those in the Cargo Selectivity System. If the entry passes the specialists' review, it is liquidated—meaning that its duties have been determined and the broker has paid the resulting bill. If the review raises questions or identifies any violations, an investigation may follow. Throughout the sometimes lengthy liquidation pro-

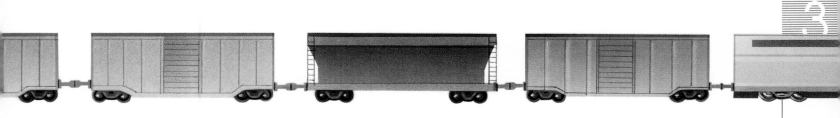

cess, the Automated Commercial System automatically fulfills the agency's reporting requirements, preparing and transmitting more than five hundred statistical summaries—daily, weekly, monthly, annually, and on demand—for Customs Service staff, the Internal Revenue Service, the Treasury Department, and other federal organizations.

FROM SHIP TO SHORE

Securing the release of cargo from the Customs Service is only the beginning of the journey from a marine terminal to inland distribution channels. Once released, each container of merchandise must be transferred from a known location—the cargo hold of a mammoth vessel—to the dock, and thence to a temporary warehouse, a truck, or a rail car bound for other parts. The job is a logistical nightmare. Containers, says one Swedish shipping executive, "tend to breed like rabbits and overflow any area if not kept under strict control." By one estimate, the unloading and transferring of a thousand containers—a typical day's work at a modern marine terminal—would entail 3,700 movements of cranes, forklifts, and other equipment. The degree to which information about containers and loading equipment flows smoothly during the operation determines whether these are 3,700 opportunities for productive effort or, as a maritime administration researcher has put it, "3,700 opportunities for mishandling, loss, or delay."

In a number of European and Asian ports, computerized information systems have proved invaluable in the effort to impose order on dockside chaos. Maritime officials have recently begun evaluating the potential use of such systems in the United States. For example, at a marine terminal in Savannah, Georgia, longshoremen who once conducted on-site inventories on the backs of envelopes have tested the use of portable computers and radios to transmit inventory data to the shipowner's host computer, which can verify unloaded cargo against the ship's manifest. The use of dockside computers provides the marine terminal operator with accurate and instantaneous data, speeding the vessel's return to sea.

At the heart of sophisticated information systems for marine terminals is the ability to automate the identification of cargo containers and the forklifts and other equipment needed for transporting them. Not only does this tech-

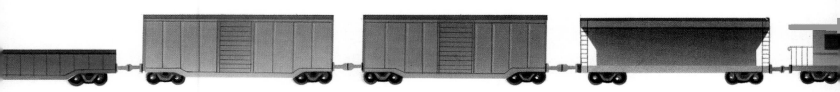

nology allow the terminal operator to know what equipment is available, it also allows the operator to know where on the grounds of the terminal the equipment or container is.

Marine officials have explored the potential of several types of location-sensing systems, from satellite relays to infrared technology. One system that seems to work well in the rough-and-tumble environment of a marine terminal employs radio-frequency microcircuitry to transmit identification data from the terminal yard to a central computer. Each container is outfitted with a transponder—an electronic device about the size of a credit card. The transponder combines a low-power radio transmitter with a small amount of memory, just enough to hold an identification number for the container and a brief list of its contents.

At dockside and at other entries and exits to the terminal, devices called interrogators continually broadcast radio signals. As a container is unloaded from a ship, for example, the signals cause the transponder tag on the container to release its information, also in the form of radio signals. The interrogator relays the data to the marine terminal's main computer, which logs the container into the terminal. During its stay there, a container commonly rests on a flatbed truck-trailer. The trailer is parked in a space equipped with a buried transponder having the parking-space number in memory.

To record the location of each container, a utility vehicle is driven along the rows of parking spaces. Mounted on the vehicle is an interrogator that asks the parking-space transponder for the space number and queries the container transponder for the container's identification number and list of contents. This information, passed to the main computer, enables terminal personnel to locate any container. When a container leaves the terminal, either by ship or by truck, the computer logs it out.

Although this level of surveillance is within reach for the maritime industry as a whole, there remains a major barrier to a widespread improvement in efficiency: the lack of common standards for automatic identification and location-sensing equipment. Each shipping line tends to have its own configuration of hardware and software for such equipment, which may not be compatible with those of another carrier or with those of the various marine terminals the carrier frequents. Despite these difficulties, optimistic observers look forward to the

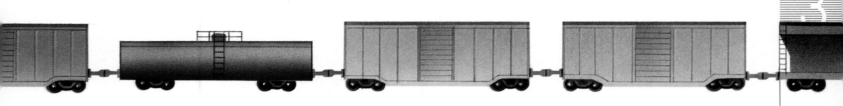

eventual integration of information processing and cargo handling, with the ultimate goal of fully automated marine-terminal operations.

THE ELUSIVE BOXCAR

Far from being unique to the unloading docks of marine terminals, the problems of standardizing computer technology—for information exchange, equipment handling, and process control—are universal among freight handlers. For railroads, the implications are continental in scope and significantly more complicated. For instance, a shipment of fruit traveling from West Coast to East may be handed off for hauling by as many as five different railroads before it reaches the marketplace. Until the advent of computers, the shipment would have left a lengthy trail of paper and required the intercession of scores of human handlers in an effort to prevent a rail car—or the entire shipment—from going astray as cars were switched from one train to another at the many intermediate stops involved in the cross-country journey.

Railroads in the United States have long viewed automation as a key to their economic survival, the means to improving not only management but hauling efficiency and labor productivity. As early as the 1920s and 1930s, railroads had begun using remote-controlled electrical relays to set rail switches, reducing the number of people required to do the job and speeding up the process in the bargain. As John E. McGinley, a railroad-yard superintendent of the Richmond, Fredericksburg and Potomac (RF&P) Railyard in Virginia, has noted, "Computers are just an improvement in the switching hardware—more powerful, with more flexibility." In the 1950s, the industry began coming to grips with the enormity of its freight- and equipment-monitoring problems by introducing computers into its information-processing systems. Partly as a result of the innovative use of computers, railroads managed to pare their labor force by two thirds over three decades: In 1955, more than one million workers were engaged in the tasks related to moving 1.3 billion tons of freight over the rails. In 1985, only 340,000 workers were required to handle virtually the same amount of cargo.

Much of what railroad employees do is to keep records of an enormous volume of dynamic information—data that changes constantly, such as the history of rail-car movements (needed to calculate rents to be paid by the hauling railroad

to the railroad that owns a given car), inventories of freight-hauling equipment, along with waybills and bills of lading—documents issued by the railroad listing a shipment's contents, its route, and various charges accruing to its account. In the 1940s, RF&P alone employed hundreds of clerks to update car traffic information in huge logbooks. Furthermore, until a federal regulation of the railroads was relaxed in 1980, the industry was also compelled to file strict and accurate accounting records with the government in order to justify the rates charged to railroad customers.

Computers helped to streamline both the record-keeping and accounting functions and, eventually, to integrate them and thereby reduce to one the number of times that information had to be keyed into the system. However, as with the more recent use of computer technology at marine terminals, standardization became an issue. In the 1950s, as the large railroads began to install computers, each hired its own experts, and each expert designed a system tailored to his own preferences. By the early 1960s, McGinley recalls, "Pride of authorship had led to divergence of systems—it was hard to get any of them to work together." Each railroad thus had to devise and maintain a library of conversion programs for translating data from each of its neighboring railroads into its own data format, as well as different communications systems for receiving the data. For the RF&P, which in 1968 was using an IBM punchcard accounting system, this meant six separate decks of IBM cards, color coded for each railroad.

Not until the 1970s did a more centralized system come into play. During that decade, the Association of American Railroads (AAR) began building a computerized network for information exchange. By the early 1980s, the various components of the network had reduced the industry's mammoth freight- and equipment-control problem to manageable proportions.

A vital segment of this system is the TeleRail Automated Information Network, or TRAIN. Now in its second generation and known as TRAIN II, the network locates and keeps track of almost two million freight cars maintained by 500 railroads on more than 200,000 miles of track. In addition, it monitors the progress of individual shipments up to the point that the rail-hauled cargo is delivered to trackside customers or transferred to trucks that carry goods to their final destinations.

Operated by Railinc, a wholly owned subsidiary of AAR, TRAIN II communicates rail-car and shipment information to major U.S. railroads, two Canadian lines, the national railway of Mexico, and also to a number of shipping companies, customhouse brokers, and manufacturing concerns, including the three largest automobile manufacturers in the United States. Under the system's vigilance, the distribution of rail cars is closely coordinated with shipper demand, each year saving the railroads some 350 million empty-car miles worth nearly 150 million dollars. Computer technology is now so integral to railroading

operations that Conrail, one of the largest freight carriers in North America, insists that all shipping information must be sent through the industry's electronic data-interchange system.

FROM ASSEMBLY LINE TO SHOWROOM

Aggressive as the railroads have been on the computerization front, the impetus for new computer applications can sometimes come from shippers. One example of this is an automated loading process jointly developed by General Motors and the Grand Trunk Western (GTW) Railroad at a highly automated Oldsmobile plant in Lansing, Michigan. The process, called extended assembly-line shipping, allows just-manufactured automobiles to be moved from the assembly line to designated rail cars for immediate shipment to the automobiles' destinations—all by means of an electronic coding and scanning system.

As an Oldsmobile-in-the-making starts down the assembly line, it is tagged with a bar-code label, alternating black-and-white stripes much like those that appear on packages of goods in supermarkets. Scanners at each work station along the assembly line read the label and transmit the automobile's identification number and its location on the assembly line to a host computer. As this information accumulates, human planners are able to project when a given vehicle will be completed and ready for loading. At the beginning of each eight-hour work shift, planners determine how many rail cars will be needed to accommodate the total number of automobiles expected to be produced by each shift. The information is transmitted to the GTW, which dispatches the necessary number of cars for assignment to the twelve tracks adjacent to the Oldsmobile facility.

After a completed automobile has undergone its final quality check, another scanner notifies the computer that the vehicle is ready for loading. The computer searches for an open slot on a rail car with a destination matching that of the automobile, and determines which of fifteen berths in the car the vehicle will occupy. The computer then causes another label to be issued for the automobile. Attached to the windshield, this label lists the new car's identification number and the track, rail car, and berth to which the vehicle is assigned. As the automobile, now with a human driver at the wheel, approaches the loading ramp, it is scanned once again, so that the computer can verify the match between automobile and rail car. As soon as the scanner records that fifteen vehicles have been loaded onto a car, the computer automatically prints the necessary shipping documents, and the car is ready to be hauled away.

Depending on an automobile shipment's final destination, its trip to a dealer's sales lot may include stops at one or more freight-classification yards, where rail cars arriving from different parts of the country are sorted, or classified, according to their destinations and then assembled into new trains for the next leg of the journey. At a large classification yard, a car carrying new Oldsmobiles will be just one of about 2,500 cars to be sorted in a day.

The process of assembling new trains, composed of cars that may have either intermediate or final destinations in common, can easily go awry, resulting in delayed or misrouted shipments. With the development of electronic communications networks like TRAIN II, however, much of the vital tracking of rail cars from one classification yard to the next—as well as the guidance of cars within a given yard—has reached a high degree of automation *(pages 79-89)*. Rail-yard computers can be programmed to troubleshoot, based on information supplied by sensors at various critical points in the yard. For example, the computer can forestall collisions—fouled tracks, in the jargon of the rail yard—by warning that a car has been slow in clearing a switch. If the rails have become fouled despite the system's best efforts to prevent such a situation, the computer can block other cars from entering that branch of track, and thus prevent damage to rolling stock and freight. In addition, systems like this have greatly speeded the sorting of cars and decreased the frequency of errors that can result in misplaced cargo. The Canadian Pacific Railroad has reported that in Toronto, freight cars spend 15 percent less time in classification than before the installation of a computerized process-control system.

Despite the tremendous strides made by the railroads to coordinate their electronic data-exchange systems, the transportation industry as a whole suffers from fragmentation. Shippers who must employ more than one mode of transportation—transferring their merchandise from rail to ship, for example, or from truck to rail—still confront tracking difficulties. Increasingly, however, systems devised for the railroads are being adapted to serve other users. To some extent shippers can dial into Railinc's electronic "post office" to find out the status of their equipment or freight. As Railinc president Henry W. Meetze has observed of the service provided by TRAIN II, "We have become an electronic window between railroads and other industries."

A Better Way
to Run
a Railroad

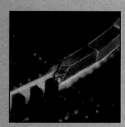

In the days before computers helped tame the complexity of the railway network, missing boxcars were the bane of the rail-freight business. Rail agents, able to draw on nothing more than handwritten logs filled with stale information, often found themselves searching frantically for hours—or even days—to locate a car that had been switched accidentally onto a wrong track.

The labyrinthine process of moving a freight car from its loading point to its destination seemed to guarantee that such disappearances would occur. During the course of a journey, the car would be coupled to many different trains; it might languish between trains, waiting in rail yards or shunted onto sidings, and if the car was traveling a great distance, it would usually roll along tracks owned by several different lines. For the railroad companies, the lost cars meant lost time, lost money, and occasionally lost customers.

Computers, with their potential for monitoring the whereabouts of every freight car in a rail network that spans the continental United States, offered a better way to run the railroads. Today, sophisticated computers can track a car through every stage of its sinuous trek from its point of origin to its destination, channeling up-to-the-minute information to all points along the line. Industry-wide data bases allow shippers, rail agents, freight-car owners, and others to enter new information or correct the old, while a computerized communication system makes the data immediately available to anyone—railroader or customer—who requests it. Pinpointing an errant freight car can now be a simple matter of summoning data to the display screen of a desktop terminal.

On the following pages, eight boxcars are traced through a typical computer-guided freighting job, exemplifying the efficiency a new technology has brought to an old pursuit.

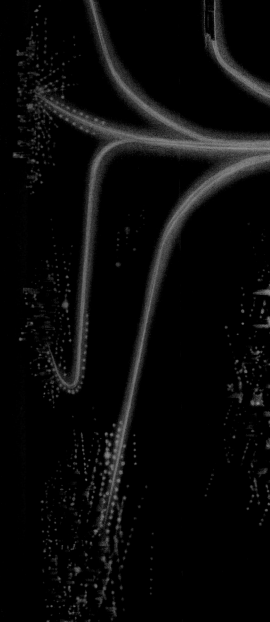

More than a hundred companies make up the Association of American Railroads (AAR). Every year, they haul nearly two million freight cars over the ribbons of track crisscrossing North America. To orchestrate the movements, the AAR uses a computer system with two key components: a data base that contains information about every freight car on the rails, and an electronic distribution network over which the information is passed from one railroad to another.

Before a new rail car leaves the assembly line, it becomes an entry in the data base—dubbed UMLER, for Universal Machine Language Equipment Register. Facts recorded include the car's type (boxcar, flatcar, hopper, and so on), dimensions, and capacity. In addition to this fixed description, UMLER records information that may vary—state of repair, availability, and usage fees. Owners update the status of their rolling stock daily, feeding UMLER hundreds of thousands

of items of new information every month.

The communications web that allows these details to be shared among the railroad companies is called the TeleRail Automated Information Network, or TRAIN. Associated with TRAIN is a data base that tells subscribers which railroad has custody of a car and also the location of a car at any moment—between cities, in a rail yard, or sidetracked. In addition, the TRAIN data base divulges whether a car is in service, in storage, or undergoing repair, whether it is full or empty, and if loaded, the nature of its freight.

Each railroad has a similar system for keeping track of freight cars within its own rail network—both those that belong to it and those of other railroads. But TRAIN, being nationwide in scope, enables the railroads to plot the step-by-step progress of a customer's cargo no matter where it goes, rendering mysterious disappearances a thing of the past.

Data Tracks
to Distant Cities

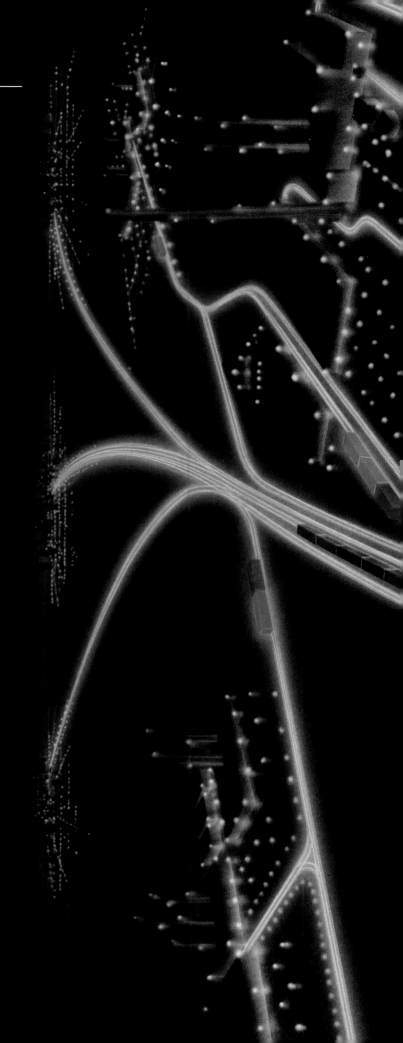

Matching Cars to Cargo

The inaugural step in any computer-controlled rail shipment is the shipper's request for freight cars. This request, sometimes made in the form of a telephone order, but more and more often transmitted by computer, specifies the number of cars desired, their type and size, where and when they are to be loaded, the cargo they will carry, and their destinations.

In many cases, however, even that level of detail does not suffice. Fragile shipments, for example, may call for boxcars with wooden floors—suitable for nailing down braces, padding, or other special cushioners—while exceptionally bulky or weighty loads may dictate heavy-duty flatcars.

At the railroad's headquarters, the customer-service representative who takes the order enters all these specifications in a computer file dedicated exclusively to that order. The representative then sends the particulars of the order through the railroad's own computer system to the car-distribution unit.

The distribution-unit manager initiates a search of the railroad's computer files to find eligible cars. If none are turned up by the survey, the search is extended to the TRAIN and UMLER data bases. The hunt is hardly a blind one; the computer can be instructed to locate not only empty cars but also cars that, though still loaded, have just reached their destinations and will soon be available for new assignments. And because the data base reveals what cargo each car last carried, the distribution-unit manager may also tailor the search to rule out any freight car that has recently carried a load incompatible with the shipper's product. A car that has just delivered a shipment of herbicides, for example, will not be slated to haul grass seed.

At the completion of its search, the computer presents the distribution-unit manager with a comprehensive list of available cars, including candidates from other rail lines. Eight cars are needed in the example chronicled here. The distribution-unit manager selects the eight that are situated closest to the shipper's warehouse (they are pictured in blue) and schedules them to arrive at the warehouse by the date noted in the computerized order.

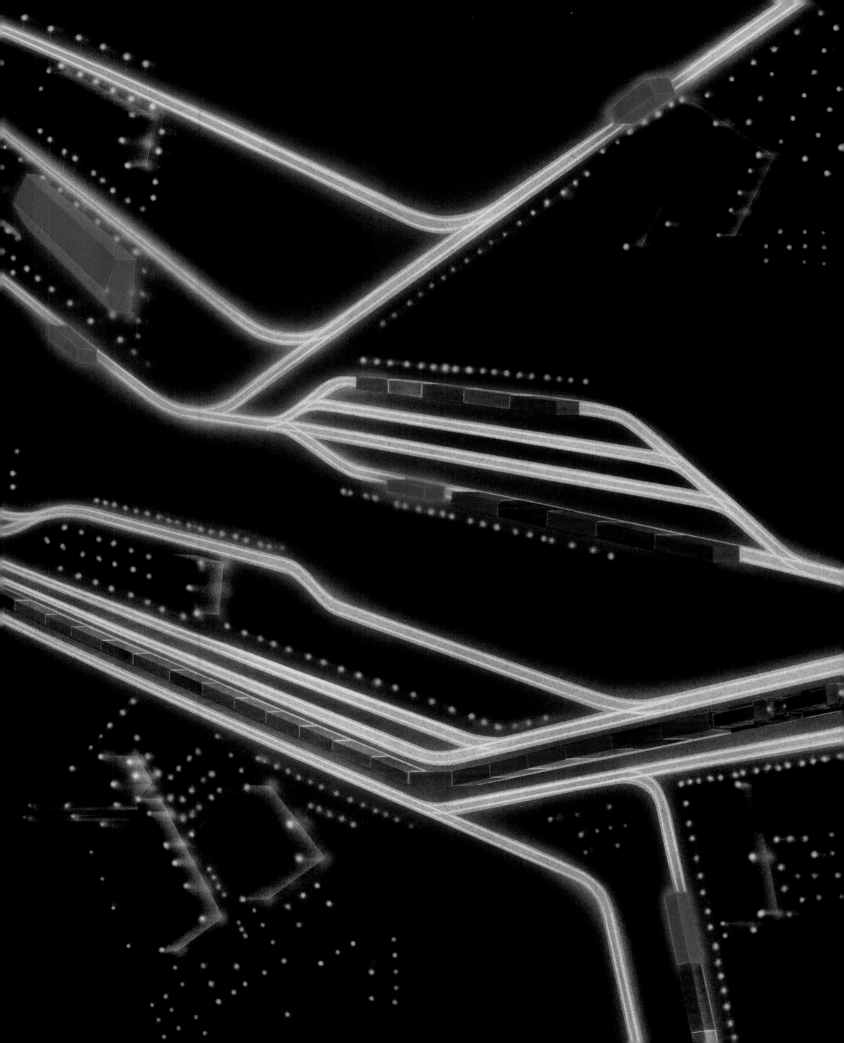

3

A Better Way to Run a Railroad

Keeping Track of Rolling Stock

Once the empty cars have been delivered to the warehouse, the shipper prepares a bill of lading for each carload of freight. This document takes an electronic form suitable for transmission from one computer to another. It describes the cargo to be loaded into each car and grants the local railroad overall authority to transport the goods and charge the shipper for the service.

Upon receiving the shipper's transmission of the bills of lading for the eight boxcars shown here, the railroad's computer automatically gen-

erates a waybill for each one. Similar to a bill of lading, a waybill describes the contents of a car, who owns it, final destination, and whether the cost of shipping has been paid in advance.

In addition, the waybill contains a rough, computer-generated itinerary for each car, specifying points at which cars are to be transferred from one railroad's jurisdiction to another's. In recommending such a route, the computer must consider any details about the goods, supplied by the shipper, that justify special handling. If the shipper informs the railroad that the cars are carrying perishable goods, for example, those cars will be sped on their way in advance of others containing nonperishables.

The software that performs the routing calculations is designed to plot the most direct path

from origin to destination. To accommodate a high, wide, or extra-heavy load, however, a human routing clerk collaborates with the computer to chart a roundabout route that circumvents a low underpass, a narrow tunnel, or an unreliable bridge that might have thwarted the car's progress. Electronic copies of the waybills are stored in each railroad's computer.

When all this planning is complete—typically, a matter of minutes—the loaded cars are ready to be hauled to the nearest rail yard (below). There, they are separated and reassembled into outgoing trains that will take them to various destinations across the continent.

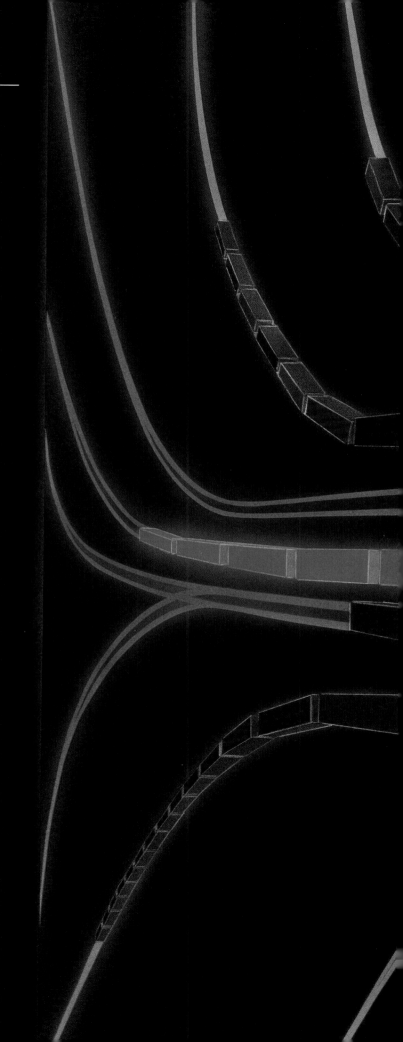

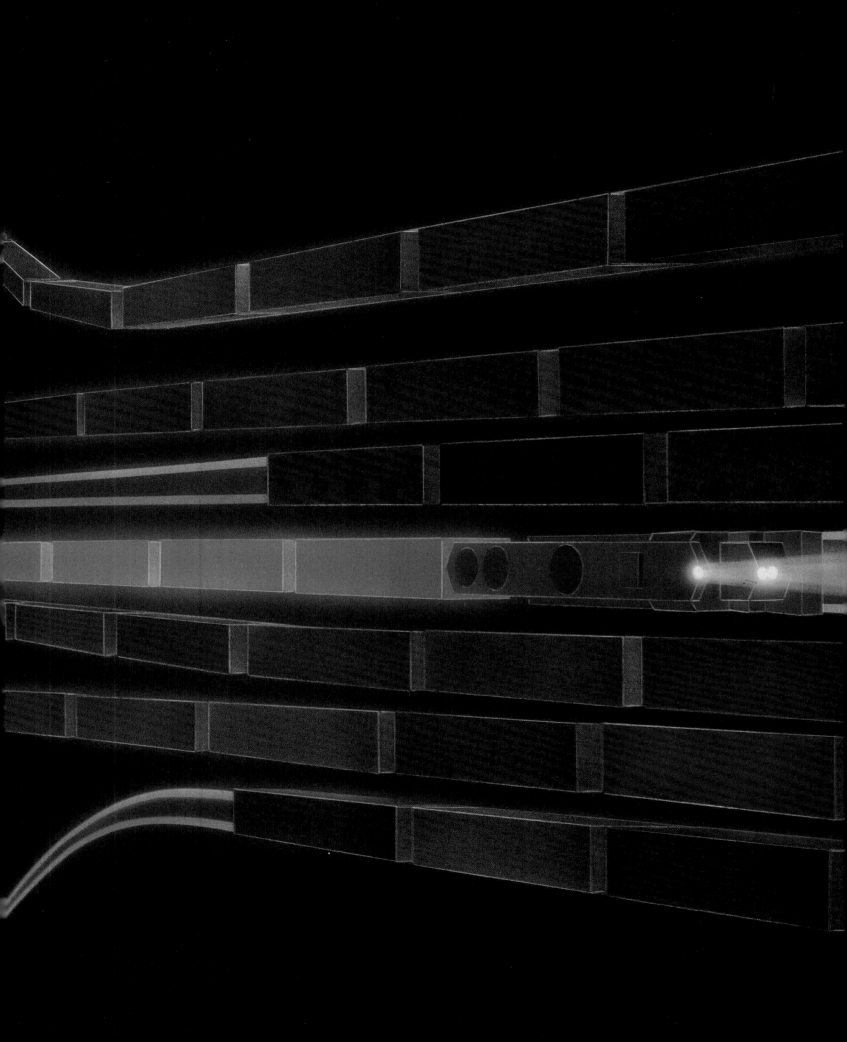

Flexible Bottlenecks

In the rail yard, the loaded cars are "humped." That is, a string of cars is nudged by a switching engine up a slight incline, or hump. At the top, one or more of the freight cars are uncoupled from the front of the string and allowed to roll down the other side of the hump through a series of switches that guide the car or cars onto the right track.

A computer at the rail yard, acting on information from the headquarters computer about the itineraries it has devised for each of the freight cars, issues a set of switch settings, called a hump list; these settings will conduct each car approaching the rail yard to the track occupied by other cars that will share the next leg of the

journey. Working from the hump list, the computer sets the switches.

The computer's duties encompass more than the mere setting of switches. As the car gains speed during its descent from the hump, for example, the computer ensures that the car will not couple too forcefully with the string of cars chosen to receive it. To accomplish this, the computer combines data about the grade, curvature, and length of each track in the rail yard with data gleaned from trackside sensors that gauge the car's speed; the computer then uses the result to activate mechanical retarders, or rail brakes, that slow the car so that it bumps the car that preceded it just hard enough to couple with it without damaging rolling stock or freight.

The computerized hump list that choreographs rail-yard operations is often improvised to some degree. A car arriving at the yard with faulty brakes or a malfunctioning coupler, for

instance, must be directed to a siding and repaired before it can join an outgoing train. The rail-yard computer keeps track of all such deviations from its hump list, preparing a second, "as-humped" list that notes the actual position of every car lined up to leave the yard.

The as-humped list is forwarded to the headquarters computer, which rearranges its electronic waybills to reflect the cars' new positions on the track. Each train assembled in the classification yard is now represented in the headquarters computer by a list of waybills. These lists are transmitted to the various rail yards down the line that are scheduled to handle the trains next. As the cars roll through successive classification yards en route to their destinations, each yard applies a similar set of computerized traffic techniques to steer them on their way.

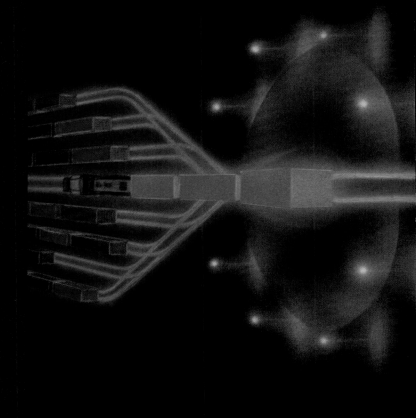

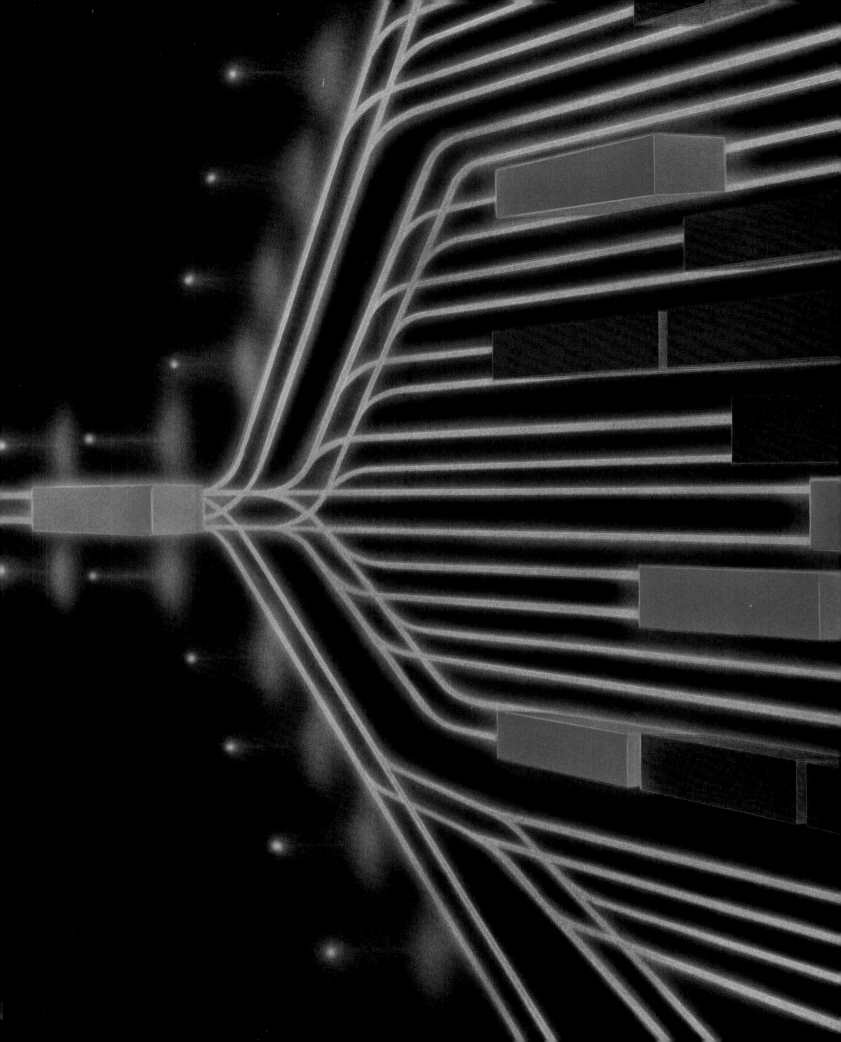

A Better Way to Run a Railroad

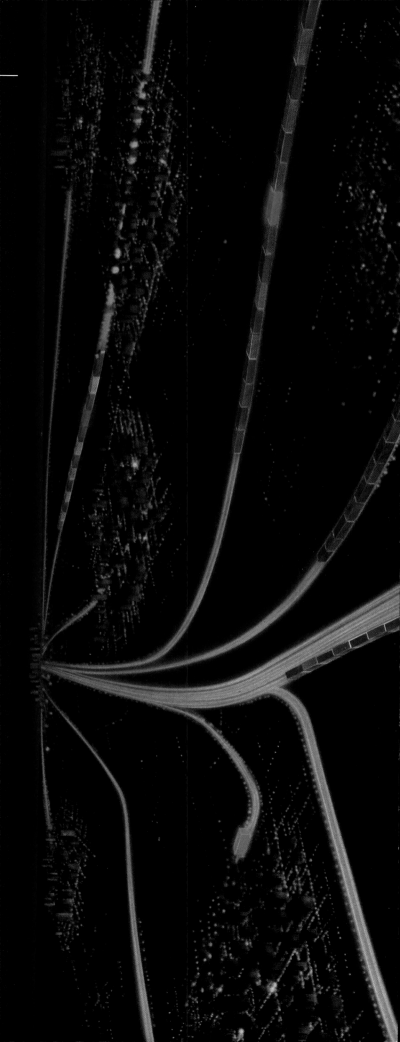

Questions and Answers

Of the eight boxcars mustered for this freighting job, three *(red)* have now reached their destinations; the other five are still in transit. Should the shipper wish to learn the status of the cargo at this point—or indeed at any moment while the shipment is under way—the railroad's computer system can supply an answer. Through the UMLER and TRAIN data bases, the computer keeps tabs on every car in every rail yard. Furthermore, the data bases are updated whenever a train stops between yards—for a change of crew, perhaps. To obtain up-to-date car-location data, the shipper need only tap into the system via telephone and modem.

With this arrangement, railroad customers can query the TRAIN data base for information about a specific car or a list of them according to the unique identification number assigned to each one. A railroad wishing to reassure a customer that a shipment will arrive as promised can ask for the car's current location and use that information to help judge whether the goods are ahead of schedule, behind it, or right on time.

As each of the eight boxcars arrives at its destination, it is unloaded and then reported empty. This information about the car's change of status is entered in the UMLER and TRAIN data bases and distributed via the TRAIN network. The boxcars are now eligible for new tasks, and the whole computerized scheduling and tracking process—having permitted not a single boxcar to be mislaid—can begin again.

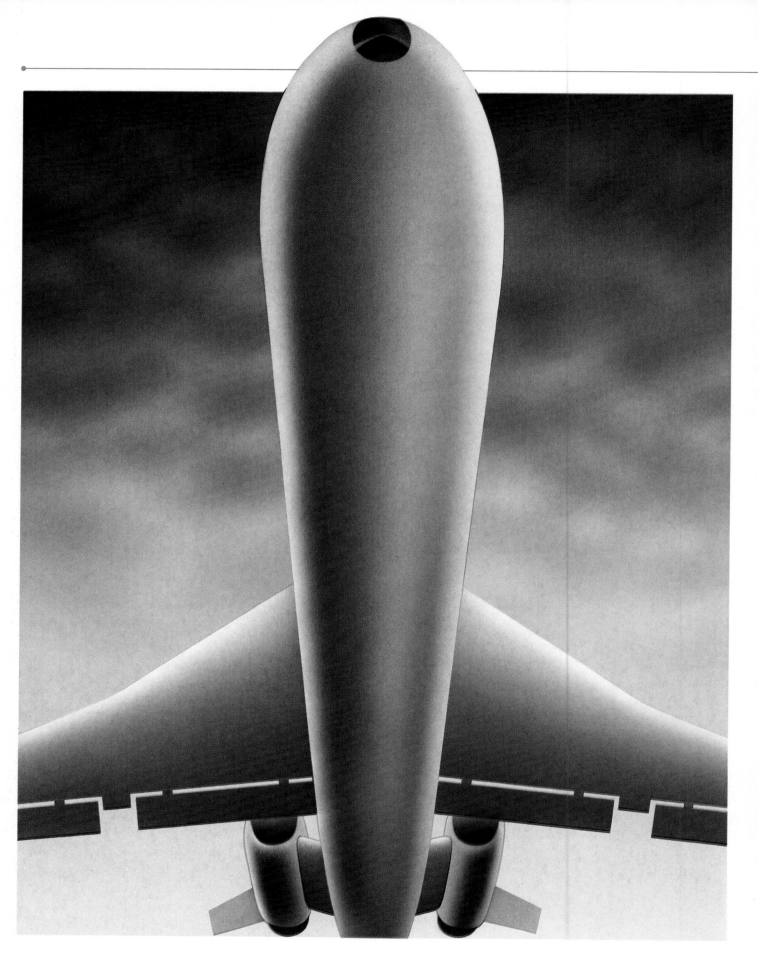

Controlling Traffic by Computer

There was nothing exceptional about the weather in the Strait of Dover on the morning of April 28, 1978. Hours earlier, a fog had rolled into this passage at the northeastern end of the English Channel, as it has most nights within seafaring memory. Even with the coming of dawn, captains sounded horns and posted extra lookouts. It was, to those experienced in Channel seamanship, business as usual. On the bridge of the 267,000-ton supertanker *Al Faiha*, fully laden with Kuwaiti crude oil destined for the refineries of Europe, all seemed well. But it was not.

Al Faiha's gyrocompass had begun to fail. Helmsmen prefer this gyroscopically stabilized instrument over a magnetic compass because it always points toward the earth's geographic north pole. Navigators call this direction true north, the direction toward the top of a chart. A magnetic compass, by contrast, points to magnetic north, which can differ from true north by as much as twenty-five degrees, depending on a ship's position. Steering by magnetic compass requires that helmsmen compensate for the variance; steering by gyrocompass does not. Unlike a magnetic compass, however, a gyrocompass is susceptible to mechanical wear and tear that can lead to inaccuracies. The problem occurs rarely, but when it does, onset is almost imperceptible. Unless the helmsmen habitually compare the gyrocompass to the magnetic one, they can be misled, sometimes into disaster.

That morning in the fog, with her helmsman's attention fixed on the failing gyrocompass, *Al Faiha* was veering off course toward Falls Bank, a dangerous shoal. If the vessel were to run aground there, she could easily break up, and the resulting hemorrhage of oil would be a major environmental disaster. Fortunately, *Al Faiha*'s waywardness had been spotted on radar in the Dover operations center of the Channel Navigation Information Service (CNIS). A traffic controller at the operations center radioed a warning to the captain, and the huge tanker returned to a safe course just ten minutes away from Falls Bank and catastrophe.

SHIPPING'S GUARDIAN ANGELS

On any day in the Dover Strait the potential for shipwreck or collision is great. Almost 600 vessels navigate these narrows every twenty-four hours. They range from tankers and dry cargo ships to dozens of ferries (including high-speed hydrofoils), fishing boats, yachts, and other pleasure craft. That they rarely collide or run aground on the strait's treacherous sandbanks is a tribute to the effectiveness of the Channel Navigation Information Service. Using shore-based radar along with computerized tracking equipment, the CNIS issues regular reports on navigation hazards to Channel traffic and provides warnings and assistance to craft in trouble—like *Al Faiha*.

CNIS is an example of a phenomenon that was unknown before the 1960s—the automated traffic-management system. Made possible by computers and

necessary by ever-increasing numbers of vehicles—automobiles and aircraft as well as ships—traffic-management systems vary widely in their details according to the speed, volume, and type of traffic being regulated. Yet all such systems have three elements in common: a means of detecting vehicles and determining their locations; one or more computers that analyze this information; and finally, a means of sending instructions and information to the operators of the vehicles.

The extent of the computer's contribution depends largely on the amount of information generated within a traffic-management system and the speed with which it must be processed. For example, the air-traffic-control system in the United States, which each year handles several million flights converging on the nation's airports at speeds up to 500 miles per hour, requires a more comprehensive use of computers than the slower and less voluminous shipping traffic managed by the English Channel's CNIS. Yet in closer quarters, such as the confines of a crowded port, the management of mere scores of arriving and departing ships can lead to the installation of computer systems with many of the capabilities of those employed in directing a skyful of airliners. And, though automobile traffic on city streets has been adequately controlled by mechanical systems since the installation of the first automatic traffic light in the 1920s, traffic engineers are using computers extensively to improve the safety and convenience of driving on urban expressways.

PERILS OF THE DEEPS AND SHALLOWS
More than 250 Vessel Traffic Systems (VTSs) like CNIS have been established worldwide, at major ports such as New York and Le Havre as well as for heavily traveled waters such as the North Sea oil fields and the Persian Gulf. On average, ships today travel twice as fast as they did fifty years ago. They transport heavier loads, and frequently their cargoes are noxious. There are more merchant vessels than ever before and, close to shore, they share navigable water with oil and gas rigs, survey ships, dredges, fishing boats, ferries, and day-sailers. Many ports have specific hazards—bridges, breakwaters, narrow channels, severe tides, or erratic currents—that demand precise navigation and coordination with other traffic.

On one level, a VTS functions as an information service to ships, passing along advisories about other traffic, weather, tides, and sea conditions, for example. On another level, VTS controllers may, under extreme circumstances such as impending collision, issue compulsory sailing instructions directly to the captain of a ship—something of a novelty in the maritime world where, by law and custom, the captain has always been the supreme authority aboard a vessel.

One of the most advanced vessel traffic systems operates in the port of Rotterdam, known as Europort. Stretching twenty-five miles along the banks of the Maas River near its mouth on the North Sea, Europort is packed with piers, docks, oil refineries, railroad yards, canals, and shipyards. When river transports, tugboats, fishing boats, and pleasure craft are counted, the harbor handles more than 300,000 vessels each year and nearly 300 million tons of cargo. To orchestrate this activity, the Rotterdam VTS relies on the data-processing capa-

bilities of computers to a degree rare in harbor-traffic control and is looked upon as a model for other ports.

The origins of the Rotterdam system lie in computerless traffic-management procedures that were inaugurated in 1956. As the port grew, the rules became increasingly complex and unwieldy, so much so that in the mid-1970s the Dutch Ministry of Transport and the City of Rotterdam decided against further tweaking of the old system and opted instead for a computerized one. Design and construction of the new system took nearly ten years and cost more than ninety million dollars.

The completed installation includes a network of twenty-eight radar stations to track and help identify ships and eight closed-circuit television cameras focused on ferry crossings and harbor entrances, of which there are several within the port. Surveillance information is fed to three manned traffic-control centers. They are responsible for directing the movements of ships within three sharply defined areas of the harbor. The three jurisdictions are further divided into sectors, each of which falls under the supervision of an individual controller.

More than 100 computers, including backup units, store and analyze the profusion of data that the Rotterdam VTS generates. Among their functions are to interpret and display radar returns and to provide up-to-the-minute reports on visibility, wind direction and strength, and tidal height, all gathered from sensors positioned throughout the harbor.

For a ship approaching Europort from the sea, surveillance begins as soon as the vessel appears on radar—as far as thirty miles outside the port limits, where it is first picked up on radar. The ship's identity is confirmed by radio and compared to a list of expected arrivals stored in the computer system's data base. This file of information also includes each ship's size, cargo, ownership, and equipment, all gleaned from *Lloyd's Register of Shipping*. Controllers place an identity label on the screen next to each ship's radar blip. This label moves along with the vessel as it approaches.

Once it is within the port, each ship is tracked continuously by at least two radar sites. Signal-processing computers combine these multiple radar views to display the ship's precise location and to distinguish it from its neighbors, no matter how close they may be. The computer system also simplifies the radar picture of the harbor by suppressing echoes from cranes, buildings, and other onshore structures that do not have an effect on port traffic. This degree of clarity and precision permits sector controllers to observe potential traffic problems and move to avert them.

Automated Commuting

Commuter rail systems move millions of people daily in hundreds of cities from Sao Paulo to Paris, and almost all rely on computers to keep things running smoothly. Computers cope admirably with the many intricacies of scheduling and train operation that a major system entails, providing safe and reliable service with a minimum of human intervention.

Typically, one central computer assumes overall management of a system, issuing commands to dozens of wayside computers that handle operations along individual portions of the line. At the start of a normal day, the central computer instructs wayside computers to follow standard procedures regarding train spacing, operating speeds, and length of sta-

Computers in charge. A modern rail transit system typically uses computers in three settings. A central computer sets schedules, dispatches trains, and monitors all activity. Wayside computers, housed at varying intervals along the track, control speed and junction settings, and ensure that trains keep a safe distance apart; computers aboard the trains put wayside commands into effect. Segmented blocks of track *(alternating purple bands)* form individual electrical circuits that are interrupted as trains pass through, allowing wayside computers to detect precisely where trains are.

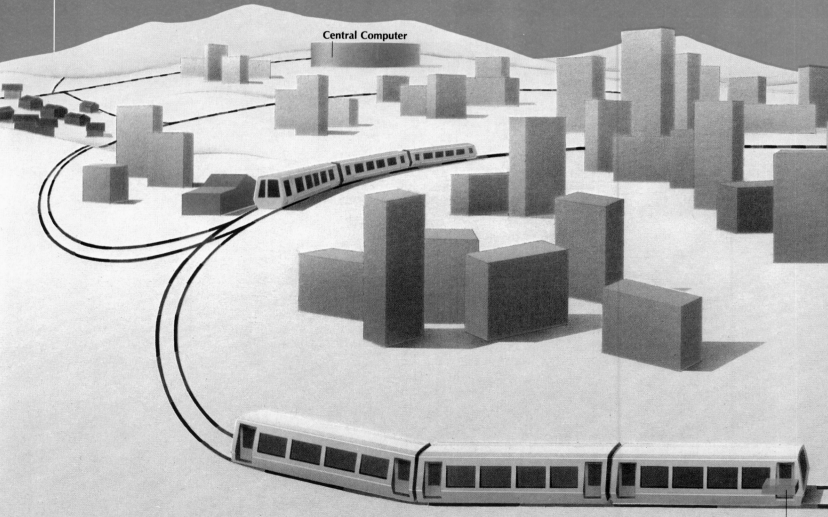

Central Computer

Onboard Computer

tion stops. It then calls for trains waiting at end-of-line stations to begin their runs at specified intervals, according to the schedule stored in its memory.

Wayside computers regulate train speeds by transmitting coded electronic signals either directly through the tracks or via a cable laid between the tracks; computers on each train pick up and decode the signals, then adjust speeds accordingly *(pages 96-97)*. The wayside computers keep tabs on train locations with information supplied by the onboard computers and by determining which block, or segment of track, a train currently occupies *(below)*.

The central computer receives continuous updates about train movements and uses the information to check for irregularities. If trains are running slightly behind or ahead of schedule, it can solve the problem on its own, directing wayside computers to speed up or slow down the appropriate trains. If the whole system is affected—by bad weather, say, or unusually heavy demand—the central computer seeks human assistance, displaying a list of possible strategies on a video screen. A supervisor could choose, for example, to adjust the run times of all trains in the system, send some to the yards, or bring idle ones into service. The computer then takes care of the details, calculating revised schedules and forwarding new commands to all wayside computers.

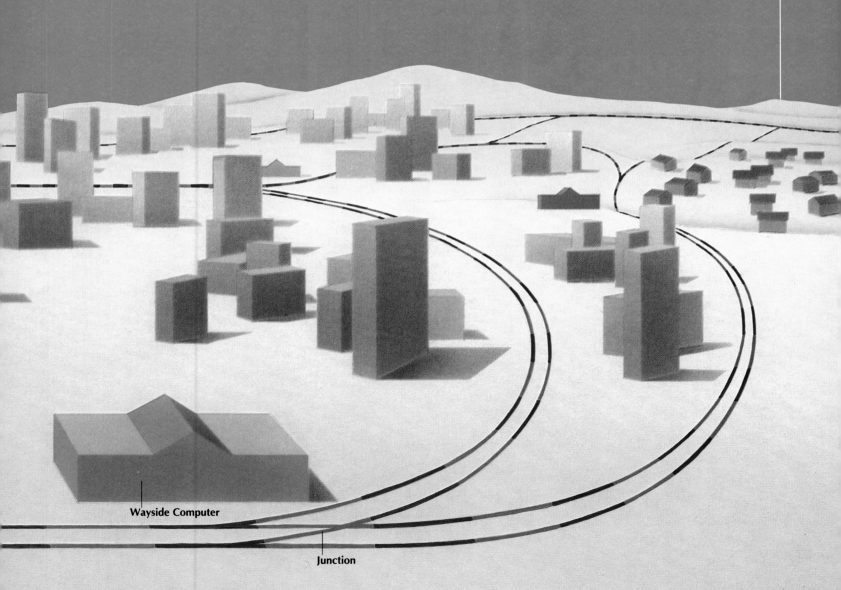

Wayside Computer

Junction

Putting a Train through its Paces

Once on its way, a train is in the hands of the many wayside computers along its path. Efficient and safe operation, especially when stopping and starting at stations, depends on a careful coordination of effort between these wayside processors and each train's onboard computing equipment.

Methods differ, but in most systems, when a train approaches a station, a sensor on the underbody of the first car detects a marker between the tracks that tells the onboard com-

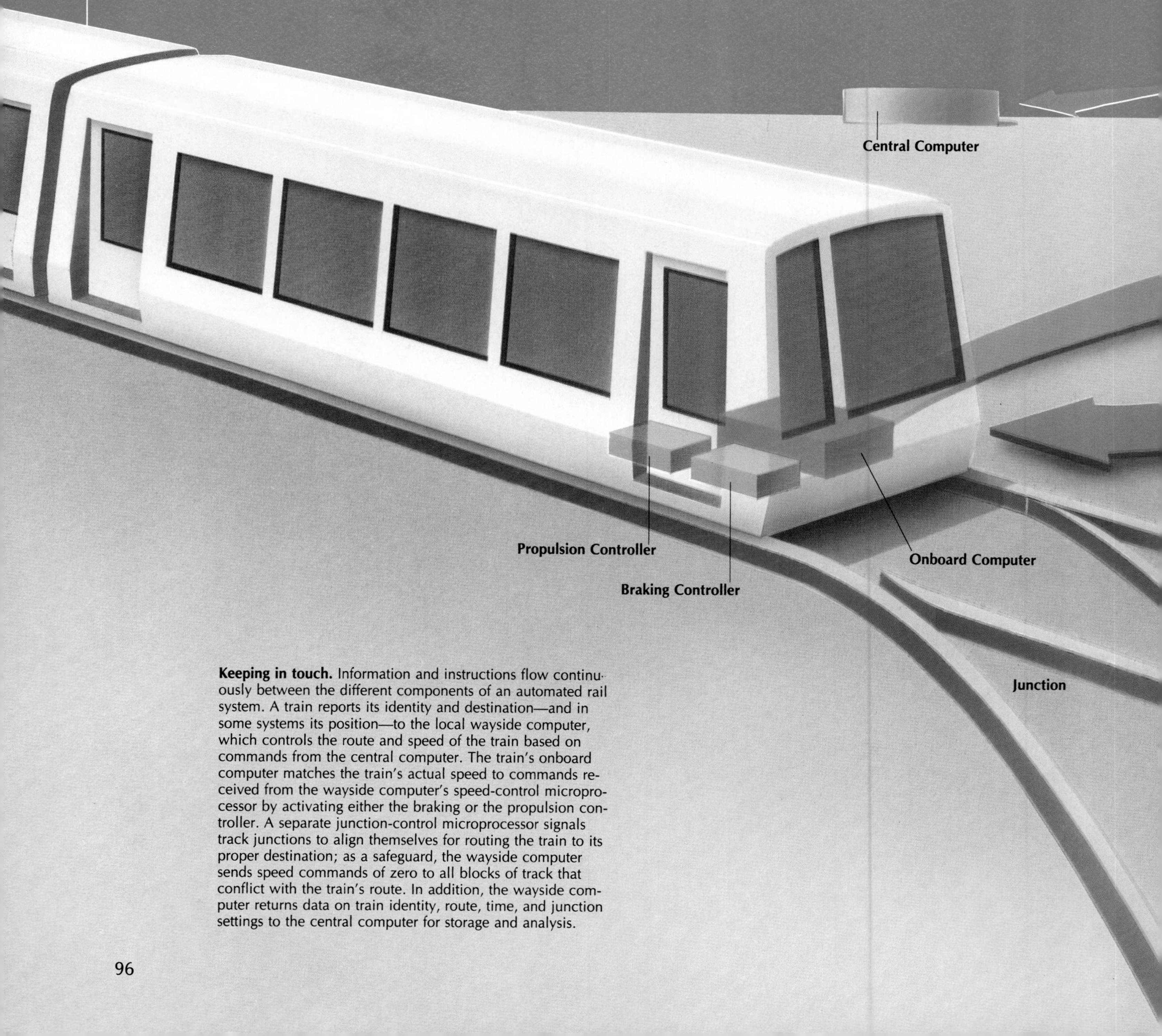

Central Computer

Propulsion Controller

Onboard Computer

Braking Controller

Junction

Keeping in touch. Information and instructions flow continuously between the different components of an automated rail system. A train reports its identity and destination—and in some systems its position—to the local wayside computer, which controls the route and speed of the train based on commands from the central computer. The train's onboard computer matches the train's actual speed to commands received from the wayside computer's speed-control microprocessor by activating either the braking or the propulsion controller. A separate junction-control microprocessor signals track junctions to align themselves for routing the train to its proper destination; as a safeguard, the wayside computer sends speed commands of zero to all blocks of track that conflict with the train's route. In addition, the wayside computer returns data on train identity, route, time, and junction settings to the central computer for storage and analysis.

puter to start slowing the train. Based on information about the train's speed, length, and load as well as the distance to the station, the onboard computer calculates exactly how much braking to apply; subsequent markers allow the computer to make adjustments so that the train comes to a smooth halt at the platform.

The onboard computer next sends a "berthed" signal to the wayside computer, which only then permits the doors to be opened. For proper scheduling, the wayside computer allows a predetermined "dwell time" to pass before it issues a new speed command to the train. The onboard computer compares the train's speed, zero in this instance, to the speed command, and detecting a difference, calls for acceleration. The train begins to move out of the station and on toward its next stop, switching over, in the process, to the control of the next wayside computer.

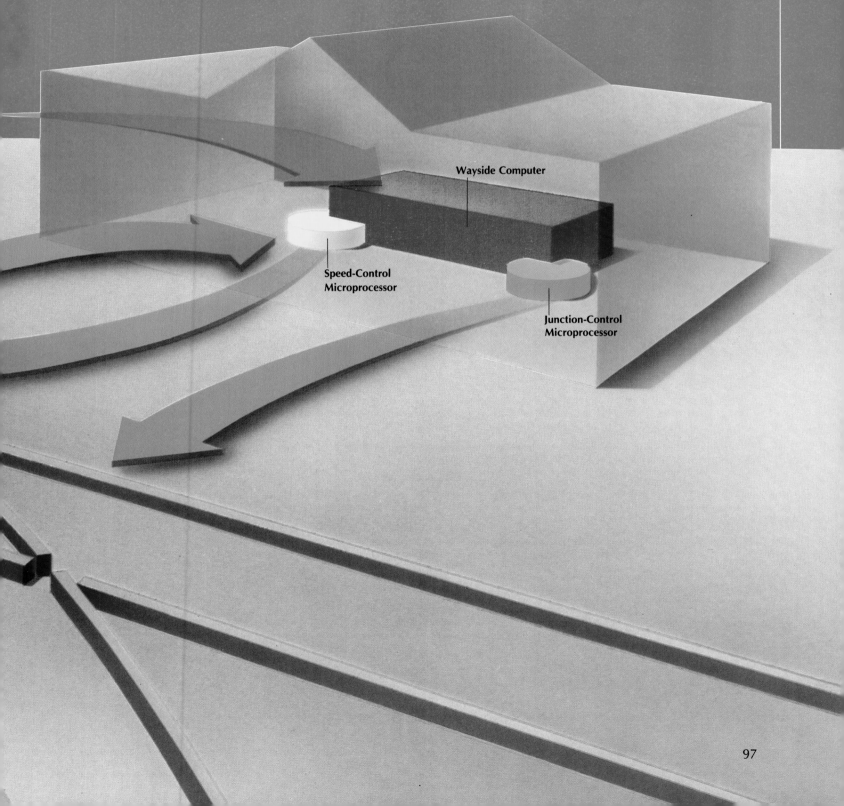

Wayside Computer

Speed-Control Microprocessor

Junction-Control Microprocessor

UP IN THE AIR

Though overlapping radar is necessary at Europort to positively identify ships that often pass within a few hundred yards of each other, in an air-traffic-control system, aircraft are so widely separated to reduce the chance of collision that single-radar coverage is enough to track them, the more so since commercial aircraft nowadays are equipped with electronic devices called transponders. Installed in an airliner or other aircraft, a transponder transmits a four-digit code as a radar beam sweeps past. On the ground, the number passes to computers that compare it with a data base correlating codes with flight numbers. Doing so ascertains the aircraft's identity, which the computer displays on the controller's radar screen.

Transponders, computers, and even radar can be considered recent improvements to air-traffic-control systems, which began humbly in the 1930s, when airline-company dispatchers became concerned about the growing number, even then, of near-collisions. With airliners from different companies approaching airports from every point of the compass—and all without any coordination whatever—only alert aircrews stood between a safe arrival or departure and disaster.

In an effort to remedy the chaotic situation, individual airlines began on their own initiative to exchange aircraft-position reports in the Chicago area. Before the effort could be widely duplicated, the next step had been taken. Early in 1936, a consortium of airlines established air-traffic-control facilities in Newark, Chicago, and Cleveland to manage the flow of air traffic into the busy terminals at those cities. In July of the same year, the federal government took over operation of this elementary system.

The first generation of air-traffic controllers relied "more on technique than technology," as one veteran remembered. The system was totally manual. Controllers posted flights on a wall-size blackboard, where revisions, additions and deletions could easily be made. Nearby, a large table map depicted cross-country air routes. Controllers placed small wooden markers—dubbed "shrimp boats" because of their shape—on the map, each one representing an airplane. A strip of paper clipped to each shrimp boat repeated much of the information that was written on the blackboard, including the airline to which the aircraft belonged, the flight number, the plane's departure time, and altitude. Later, the solid blackboards were replaced by strips of similar material that were easily rearranged in order to maintain a chronological list of current and planned flights.

Airline dispatchers required their pilots to report the position of their aircraft every few minutes. Upon receiving such an update, the dispatcher passed the information by telephone to the air-traffic-control center monitoring the flight, where controllers advanced the appropriate shrimp boat. If a controller discovered two aircraft headed toward each other, he telephoned one of the airliner's dispatchers, who relayed instructions to the pilot to change altitude, enter a holding pattern, or simply to watch for the other aircraft.

The boom in air travel that followed World War II began to tax this labor-

intensive system. The number of airliners in the United States grew from 260 in 1938 to 1,480 in 1956. By then, there also were 60,000 private and company-owned planes and 23,000 military aircraft. Airplanes were flying faster. The most popular airliner before the war, the 182-mile-per-hour Douglas DC-3, was replaced by the 265-mile-per-hour DC-6.

ELECTRONIC EYES ON THE SKIES
By the mid-1950s, however, radar had become part of the air-traffic-control system, first in a simple form that showed aircraft as nothing more than bright spots on a radar screen. To create a shrimp-boat identity for any of these radar blips, a controller had to instruct pilots in a series of turns that, by their sequence, would clearly identify a blip as a particular aircraft.

Then, during the late 1950s, the airborne radar beacon appeared. Now called a transponder, this device made each plane show up on radar as a single or double slash. The pilot, when requested by a controller, pressed a button in the cockpit to make the beacon transmit an identity number that had been assigned earlier. In response to the signal, the slash marks representing the aircraft on the radar screen momentarily brightened, identifying the plane to the controller. By showing actual positions of aircraft, radar permitted them to fly closer together than had been safe when controllers predicted airplane locations based on speed and direction of flight. In effect, closer spacing increased the aircraft-handling capacity of air routes, and unequivocal identification eliminated the need for controllers to have pilots zigzag across the sky in order to identify themselves.

Despite these advances, shrimp boats and paper strips were still used to convey the speed, altitude, and destination of each flight. But instead of pushing the shrimp boats across a map, controllers nudged them across Navy-surplus radar screens, each about two feet in diameter and set into a tabletop, that had once served aboard U.S. warships to track the movements of vessels nearby. A controller still spent three-quarters of the time positioning shrimp boats,

preparing and updating flight strips, and talking on the radio with pilots and with neighboring controllers as a plane was handed from one to the next along its route. This left precious little time for a controller's most important contribution—thinking ahead to anticipate problems before they developed into dangerous situations.

The state of the air-traffic-control system as it existed in the late 1950s was adequate for aircraft of the piston-engine era. But the jet age was approaching. Almost overnight, it would seem, the airliner nearly doubled in speed to 500 miles per hour. Especially in the United States, airplanes began to replace trains as the preferred mode of long-distance transportation, and the numbers of airliners increased accordingly.

DATA PROCESSING TO THE RESCUE

To keep pace with these changes, the Federal Aviation Agency (FAA) turned to computers—for processing information more quickly than before, for help in visualizing aircraft flying through three-dimensional space, for assistance in detecting when one aircraft heads into the path of another, and for relief from the burden of paperwork. For computers to accomplish what federal aviation authorities expected of them, they would have to be programmed to perform a wide variety of tasks.

To begin with, they would be required to store each airliner's flight plan—a detailed description of the route that a plane will take on the way to its destination—in a data base for ready access. From this information, the computer would be able to generate up-to-date flight-data strips, relieving air-traffic controllers of the job.

But the data strips would serve only as backup in case of computer failure, and shrimp boats, with their paper pennants, would become obsolete. The computer would calculate an aircraft's speed and course from a sequence of radar observations and display that information, along with the aircraft's altitude as transmitted by an improved transponder, directly on the radar scope. When fully operational, the computers were expected to maintain a master list of all flights into and out of a control center's airspace and to automatically coordinate the hand-off of an airliner from one controller to another as it crossed an air-traffic-control boundary.

Accomplishing these goals would not be simple. To begin with, a suitable computer had to be found. Two computers nominated in the early 1960s, one of which was the heart of the U.S. Air Forces SAGE (Semi-Automatic Ground Environment) air-defense radar network, were both rejected because they were built with vacuum tubes, which were too slow in their calculations, too unreliable, and too costly to maintain. For most of the decade, Federal Aviation Agency personnel and computer manufacturers wrestled with the design of the system—and with each other. "Programmers complained that airplanes flew at different speeds," recalls one FAA official of the time. If they would all fly at the same speed, the programmers seemed to wish, then the software difficulties could be more easily overcome. For their part, aviation regulators complained that the computer suppliers seemed unable to understand their need for a system that would malfunction far less frequently than was customary for computers of the day.

A GIANT STEP IN RELIABILITY

Nevertheless, in 1967 the system prototype was installed in Jacksonville, Florida. It was based on an IBM Model 360 mainframe computer that the manufacturer had modified to possess an ability, unexcelled at the time, to automatically diagnose its own computer-hardware problems and reroute data for processing through backup equipment kept at the ready. IBM rechristened the computer the 9020. Not until 1975, after more than 475,000 program instructions had been tested and debugged, did all twenty of the en route control centers in the continental United States, which track airliners cross-country, have a 9020 and its software installed and running. By that time, the government had spent more than $640 million on computers and allied equipment for the FAA. By 1980, when computerized systems had been extended to approach-control centers serving airports large and small, the investment in automation had risen to exceed one billion dollars.

In the end, every goal for the system was met. Flight plans were stored in a data base according to an airplane's scheduled departure time. As the hour for takeoff approached, the computer at each control center automatically retrieved the flight plans of the flights it would handle, added the flights to a sequential list of upcoming activity, and printed data strips for the traffic controllers. Just as planned, the transponder aboard an airplane transmitted its altitude and the identity code that enabled the computer to display pertinent flight information on the radar scope.

A hand-off between controllers could be accomplished by pressing a few buttons, without the distraction of a telephone conversation. As a flight ended, the computers once again updated the list of upcoming flight activity for every control center. As a result of building self-diagnostic capabilities into the 9020, most computer crashes lasted less than a minute; longer breakdowns, ranging from a few minutes to more than an hour, occurred, on the average, every twenty-five days.

Whenever a computer malfunctioned, whether it was off-line for one minute or sixty, controllers were abruptly whisked back in time to an earlier age in air-traffic control. Even though the radars continued to function, the blips displayed on the screen suddenly lost their computer-generated identity tags. Controllers quickly rotated the radar screens to a horizontal position, set down

plastic shrimp boats, and wrote flight numbers and other information on the shrimp boats in grease pencil, which also was used to mark each aircraft's track across the screen.

These circumstances could be unnerving. A jet airliner might travel ten miles or more before a controller could positively reidentify all the blips on the radar screen. On a high-altitude flight during a period of light traffic, the chance of an accident was remote. But in a congested area such as Los Angeles or New York, for example, controllers had to work at top speed, and flight crews had to be doubly alert to assure that all aircraft would remain a safe distance from each other. The return of the computers to their duties was cause for a deep sigh of relief.

Appreciating the need for a remedy, the FAA developed a computerized backup system called the Direct Access Radar Channel, or DARC. Installed in the late 1970s, DARC consisted of an independent computer at each control center that would serve as a backup for the 9020 there. The control center's radar feeds aircraft location and altitude information to both computers simultaneously. Should the 9020 malfunction, a controller can connect his radar console to the DARC computer with the flip of a switch.

DARC does not offer all the features of the 9020 system. Gone from the radar screen, for example, are numbers showing the speed of an aircraft. But

Fully automated commuter trains in Lille, France, operate safely and efficiently without drivers. Computers keep track of the trains' locations and regulate both acceleration and braking to keep trains running at one-minute intervals during rush hour. Closed-circuit television screens, a rail-system diagram, and computer consoles at a control center *(left)* allow supervisors to respond quickly to any malfunction, security problem, or even a need for additional capacity; by remote control, they can bring more cars into service to meet unanticipated demand.

the backup system adequately performs all the essential tracking functions of the 9020, with each radar blip retaining an identifying data block. Originally, DARC could display only the aircraft's flight number, but gradual improvements in the system have resulted in the addition of information about altitude and ground speed. Best of all, the radar screen remains in a vertical position, and the plastic shrimp boats stay in the drawer.

SOFTWARE BALM FOR CONTROLLERS' HEADACHES

As DARC was being installed, air traffic continued to grow rapidly. Between 1975 and 1980, the number of airline flights increased by more than 500,000 annually, a volume that once again threatened to overwhelm controllers. To extend the assistance that was offered by the computer equipment already on-line, additional programs were written. Conflict-alert software relieved controllers of having to judge whether two aircraft were in danger of colliding; the program enabled the computer to continuously calculate aircraft flight paths and warn controllers when planes were on a potential collision course. One program even alerted the controller if an aircraft flew below the minimum safe altitude for a route.

Safety considerations led the FAA to save on magnetic tape a record of all activity in the air-traffic-control system, so that the flight paths of aircraft involved in accidents could be reconstructed. This practice enabled controllers to review their performance and to conduct training exercises based on real flight situations. Another program in the same spirit, officially called the "quality assurance patch" by the FAA and nicknamed "the snitch" by controllers, prints a report for supervisors that details the occasions when controllers have permitted planes to approach each other too closely.

Yet the very improvements in software that helped better the performance of controllers also taxed the computers' capacity, making the entire system less responsive. By 1985, for example, the radar display of aircraft movements on a very busy day could lag behind reality by as much as fifteen seconds, time enough for an airliner to travel two miles. On such occasions, when radar

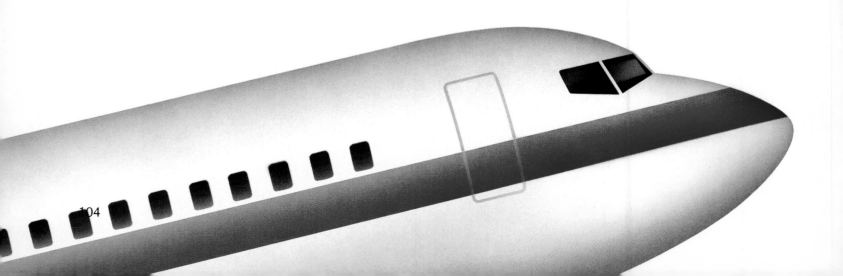

displays became a window into the recent past rather than a view of the present, some controllers called on the services of DARC. The backup system's limited capabilities were more than compensated for by the up-to-date picture of the air-traffic situation that it provides.

Furthermore, the system suffered from a rigid design. For example, each en route center and approach-control facility was self-contained and independent of every other. Such an approach was a simple way to guarantee that a computer glitch at one location could not affect operations at another, but it also prevented an especially busy facility from ''borrowing'' computer capacity by transferring part of the workload to a less burdened control center.

THE NEXT GENERATION

The inevitable had begun to happen. Just as burgeoning air traffic had swamped the manual control system in the late 1950s, ever-increasing numbers of flights in the 1980s were threatening to overload the computerized system that had been established during the preceding decade. There was only one remedy, to replace the old system with a new one—better computers, upgraded software, and additional capabilities. It would be known as the Advanced Automation System, or AAS.

Installation of the AAS is to be completed in stages by the turn of the century. A transitional first stage, completed in 1989, involved the replacement of control centers' aging IBM 9020 computers with IBM 3083s. These machines are capable of running the same software used with the 9020, but at ten times the speed. At that rate, even the busiest en route center needs no processing assistance from its neighbors, except in the unlikely event of a fire or an explosion that brings down all of a center's computers at once. To counter such a catastrophe, the 3083s are linked in a communications network, an arrangement made possible by techniques established since the 1960s for safeguarding computers from each other while permitting them to exchange data. In the event that one of the en route centers is put out of commission, other centers can instantly shoulder the load.

When AAS is complete, it will relieve the 3083 host computers of responsibility for the job of continuously updating all of the system's radar screens; each display will be managed by its own, smaller computer, which will receive aircraft-tracking information from the host. Accomplishing this will require at least 100,000 additional lines of program instructions, bringing the total to nearly 600,000. Eventually, the 3083s are to be replaced by computers programmed with new air-traffic-control software. Together hardware and software will operate fast enough that the system should be able to handle any increase in the numbers or speed of aircraft that may occur while yet another generation of equipment is planned.

ON THE ROAD TO EASIER DRIVING

The problems of managing air traffic resemble, in some ways, those that confront architects of traffic-management systems for city streets and for the multilane arteries that conduct high volumes of traffic deep into the hearts of urban centers. For example, because all aircraft pilots heading in either direction between two points generally prefer to fly the shortest distance, these straight-line airways define traffic patterns in the sky almost as rigidly as roads do on the ground. For both kinds of traffic, engineers must devise methods for regulating the space between vehicles so that travel remains as safe as possible and the inconvenience of delays is minimized.

Computers have made traffic lights smarter. Whereas the proportion of red to green at each intersection was once controlled by clocks that operated independently of one another, that job is now often coordinated by computers. Sensors buried under the surface of the roadway monitor the number of vehicles passing in different directions through intersections and pass the information to the computers, which are programmed to adjust stop time and go time to facilitate the flow of traffic.

There is a limit, however, to the practicality of stopping all the vehicles traveling in one direction for the benefit of traffic moving in another. The solution, of course, was the limited-access highway, with cloverleaf intersections and traffic signs printed with the words "merging traffic." In rural and many suburban areas, traffic is light enough that entering the flow presents little difficulty. But in large cities where expressway traffic can barrel along almost bumper-to-bumper, joining the stream can be an exercise in frustration. Traffic backs up on entry ramps as drivers hesitate. Stopped vehicles block adjacent intersections. Gridlock threatens.

UP-TO-DATE IN CHICAGO

Chicago offers an example of how valuable computers can be in keeping freeway traffic moving. Traffic engineers there began using computers in 1962 to gather data on traffic flow along a section of the ten-mile-long Eisenhower Freeway, a six- and eight-lane artery that speeds traffic from the suburbs west of Chicago toward the center of the city. Since then, Chicago has computerized its entire 110-mile freeway system.

Induction detectors, which sense the presence of the iron and steel, monitor

the passage of vehicles at three-mile intervals in most lanes; one lane in each direction on every road is monitored every half mile. Sensors are also installed at entry and exit ramps. Altogether, the pulse of traffic is taken at 1,600 points throughout the highway network.

A detector, during the instant a car takes to cross it, generates a current that signals the presence of a vehicle to a central computer of the kind used to control steel- and paper-manufacturing processes. As often as sixty times a second, the computer checks each detector in the system for the presence of a vehicle. By keeping track of this information, the computer can calculate the volume of traffic in vehicles per hour at those points.

Furthermore, as the computer polls each detector, it notes the percentage of time that it senses the presence of a vehicle, a factor that traffic engineers call lane occupancy. Engineers have found that 20 percent lane occupancy—the equivalent of 20 percent of the road's length being occupied by vehicles, or four car lengths between vehicles—is ideal, permitting the greatest number of vehicles to travel at the speed limit. Sections of freeway that are operating at or below 20 percent occupancy are displayed in green on an electronic map at traffic-control headquarters. Between 20 percent and 30 percent occupancy, where the gap between vehicles is little more than two car lengths, traffic speed decreases as drivers find it difficult to change lanes, and the danger of rear-end collision rises. This condition is displayed as yellow on the system map. Above 30 percent occupancy the display changes to red; the road is considered officially "congested."

The computer continuously compares differences in occupancy between adjacent sections of roadway. Should the difference exceed a preselected percentage, indicating an obstruction to traffic—a disabled vehicle or an accident, for example—the computer pinpoints the problem zone on the map. A dispatcher directs a patrolling road-service emergency truck to the scene to render assistance if possible or to summon a police car, fire engine, or ambulance when necessary. Meanwhile, the computer reduces the press of traffic near the delay by altering the timing of traffic signals on entry ramps that admit one car at a time to the freeway at a rate set by the central computer in response to traffic conditions.

Warning of the tie-up is also flashed to traffic heading toward the obstruction by means of electronically controlled signs mounted above the highways. Within minutes, a traffic-congestion report is printed or displayed on computer monitors in the newsrooms of radio and television stations throughout the Chicago area so that traffic reporters can spread word of the delay and advise motorists to choose alternate routes.

To the motorist, the computers of Chicago's freeway system pass largely unnoticed, as do those that enable the automobile engine to run smoothly, efficiently, and largely free of pollution. In those two applications alone, computers used in transportation process uncountable numbers of bits. Add to them the copious streams of data zipping from stem to stern aboard ships to control engines, distribute ballast, and even to set sails; the information exchanged by computer in the business of importing and shipping goods; the contributions of computers' ability for rapid calculation to the convenience, speed, and accuracy of navigation—and a remarkable picture of modern transportation begins to emerge.

On the outside, transportation appears much the same as it has for the last twenty-five years—ships float, airplanes fly, cars and trains roll along the highways and the rails. But beneath the surface, it marches to the beat of a new drummer, the microsecond count of the computer.

Safeguards in the Sky

Over the past decade, more and more commercial aircraft have crowded into the U.S. skies and tested the traffic-juggling ability of the country's airports: Chicago's O'Hare Airport, for example, has to handle almost three takeoffs or landings each minute during peak hours. The system that keeps these and thousands of other aircraft flying safely is an ever-expanding combination of people and electronics called the National Air Space System. Operated by the Federal Aviation Administration (FAA), it presently includes some 16,000 human controllers, more than 400 airport control towers, 20 en route air-traffic-control centers dotted about the countryside, some 1,000 radio navigation aids, nearly 250 radars, and hundreds of computers.

On the ground, the computers of this national network keep track of voluminous radar, weather, and flight data and also pass information between controllers. A program called en route metering advises controllers how best to ease congestion in heavily traveled parts of the sky. Aboard an aircraft, other computers operate storm- and collision-warning radars.

Mostly, the computers of the National Air Space System guide human decisions, but some are capable of more. One is the Air Traffic Control System Command Center computer. Installed in the FAA building in Washington, D.C., it helps to ease traffic jams by forecasting the flow of planes into the nation's forty busiest airports *(page 115)*. When the computer projects that more planes are scheduled to reach an airport than air-traffic controllers there can accommodate, controllers in Washington delay the departures of some planes headed for that airport. By the mid-1990s, controllers will have gained enough experience so that the computer can be programmed to do this automatically.

Faster computers and more powerful software will automate even more of the decision-making process. A new $4-billion-plus system, called the Advanced Automation System, will be programmed to optimize flight plans for weather and air-traffic conditions. The new equipment will relieve human controllers of routine monitoring duties so that they can spend more time watching for out-of-the-ordinary events that signal danger. Not only will this system make flying even safer than it is today, but by reducing fuel consumption, it has the potential to make air travel more economical.

Boundaries Overhead

Where there was once complete flying freedom for aviators, pilots today operate under strict rules and procedures, all based on a carefully segmented view of the country's skies. The National Air Space System divides the aerial realm into two basic categories: areas of positive control, where aircraft are directed by air-traffic controllers; and areas in which aircraft generally fly unsupervised.

Areas of less stringent control are defined by exception. They comprise all altitudes below 18,000 feet that also lie

7,000 Feet

2,500 Feet

1,400 Feet

outside special regions called Terminal Control Areas (TCAs), surrounding the busiest airports in the United States. A TCA may extend as high as 7,500 feet and have a radius, depending on altitude, of up to fifteen miles.

Within TCAs—and above 18,000 feet between them—lies positive-control airspace. There, virtually every move an airplane makes, from the time it takes off until it lands at its destination, is dictated by ground controllers following the flight's progress on radar.

24,000 Feet

18,000 Feet

En Route Center

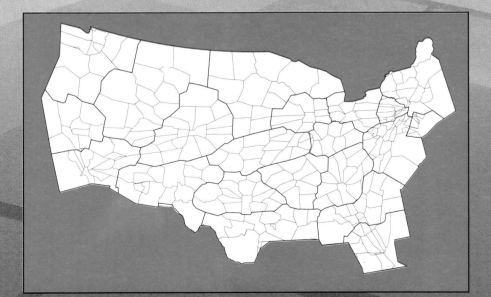

A structured airspace. The positive-control TCA above an airport *(purple)*, has the shape of an upside-down wedding cake to conform with the paths of incoming and outgoing flights. The busy airport at left has a three-tier TCA; the less congested installation at far right has a two-tier version. A cube of space *(yellow)*, called terminal airspace, surrounds a TCA and extends to an altitude of 10,000 feet or more. This cube marks the boundary of the area monitored by terminal airspace controllers. When a plane leaves the terminal airspace, it comes under jurisdiction of an en route center, which regulates traffic flying outside terminal airspaces. These intercity regions are divided horizontally and vertically into sectors. On the map at right, thick black borders show the areas covered by en route centers for altitudes between 24,000 feet and 35,000 feet; sector boundaries are outlined by thinner lines.

From Departure Gate to Takeoff

Before taking off for a flight through positive-control airspace, a pilot submits to the nearest en route-center computer a flight plan, which specifies estimated departure and arrival times, cruising altitude, and the navigational aids that the plane will travel past. Upon approval by air-traffic-control personnel, this information is relayed to computers in the airport control tower, and also to the computers of other en route centers along the way and those of the destination airport. The information, which will be updated at takeoff and during the trip, is stored in the memory of these computers and

Tag for a flight. A data strip for a Washington-New York flight specifies (in blocks from left): Eastern Airlines flight 1402; Boeing 727 with an altitude-reporting transponder; computer file 858; transponder code 0537; proposed (P) departure time, 1100 Universal Time (7 AM EDT); requested altitude, 190 (19,000 feet); originating at DCA (Washington National Airport) and following a route from DCA to MITCH intersection and route V445, then to navigation beacon DQO and on to New York, following an approach procedure called NANC 11 to land at LGA (LaGuardia).

EA 1402	0537	DCA	DCA MITCH V445 DQO NANC 11			
B727/A	P1100		LGA			
858	190					

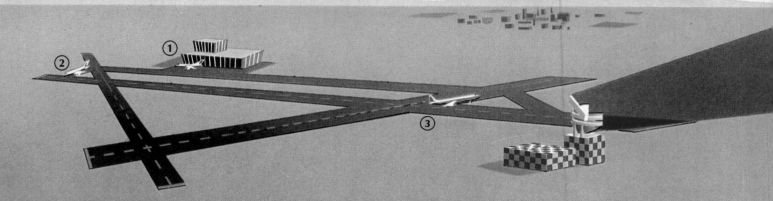

1. Preparing for takeoff. At the gate, the copilot radios the clearance-delivery controller, who tells the cockpit crew of any changes in the flight plan, such as delays caused by congestion. The controller, one of many in the airport tower, issues a transponder code and departure radio frequency, and designates a runway.

2. Taxiing to the runway. The copilot, using the departure radio frequency, now contacts the ground controller, who ensures safe and orderly transit from the gate to the runway. After surveying the traffic, the controller assigns the aircraft a taxiway route to the runway and gives permission to leave the departure gate.

3. Taking off. After the aircraft has taxied into the "number one for takeoff" position, just off the active runway, the plane is "handed off." Jurisdiction is transferred to a local air-traffic controller, who visually surveys the sky and clears the flight for takeoff. The pilot then accelerates down the runway.

4. Entering radar control. Departure-control radar *(violet)* picks up the plane when it flies into radar coverage near the end of the runway. The radar reveals the craft's position relative to other planes in the area, but the local controller continues to follow the flight visually until relieved of the responsibility by a departure controller.

printed out by each of them in the form of a flight-data strip *(below, left)*. The strips serve traffic controllers as a backup to the electronic system.

With all the necessary data at hand, successive controllers *(bottom, left)* grant clearance for the plane to taxi and to take off. Then radar begins tracking it. At this point, the flight becomes the responsibility of the departure controller. An aircraft shows up on departure-control radar as a letter denoting the work station of the controller who is assigned to the flight. One plane is distinguished from another by a signal from a transponder, an electronic device in the airplane that is triggered by radio signals from the ground to broadcast a code that identifies the flight and, depending on the type of transponder, reports the plane's altitude. Displayed on the radar screen along with the speed of the aircraft as calculated by computers located on the ground, the transponder data enables the departure controller to direct a plane through the terminal airspace. Before an airliner exits terminal airspace, responsibility for the flight is passed along to the nearest en route center.

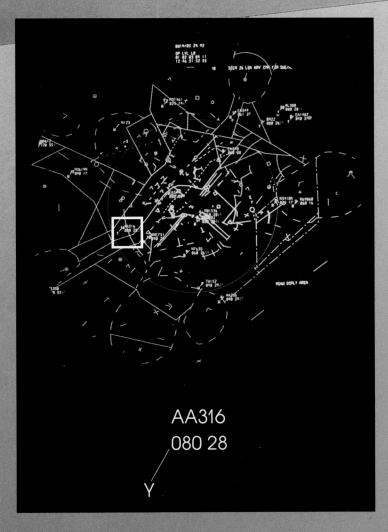

What the controller sees. The departure controller's radar screen *(upper right)* displays a complicated pattern of straight solid lines, which divides the local airspace; dashed circles, which mark possible holding patterns; and small squares and circles, which depict navigational aids—all overlaid by data blocks of numbers and letters, which denote specific flights. This overall view indicates nineteen flights approaching or departing New York's John F. Kennedy Airport around noon on a typical day. The data block outlined by the white box is enlarged at lower right to show information about a single flight: American Airlines Flight 316, flying at 8,000 feet (080) and 280 knots (28), under the supervision of the controller assigned to work station Y.

AA316
080 28

Y

A Cross-Country Relay

Within five to ten minutes after takeoff, jurisdiction over a flight in positive-control airspace passes from the departure controller to an en route-center controller. That controller may follow a flight through one or more of the blocks, or sectors, into which the airspace is divided *(below)*, depending on traffic and distance. Then the flight is handed off to another controller in the same en route center or in the next one along the route. This relay of a flight from one controller to another continues until the plane nears its destination,

Dividing the skies. How the controlled airspace above 18,000 feet is sectored for radar surveillance is diagrammed here. Hundreds of sectors are layered above the United States, each several thousand feet high and up to 200 miles wide. Many sectors fall under the control of a single en route center. While some commercial traffic flies in the lowest two horizontal flight levels, most jets use the top layer, which begins at 35,000 feet and extends indefinitely from there. Supersonic planes may fly at 55,000 feet, while subsonic airliners generally cruise around 39,000 feet.

when control passes to an approach controller, who handles arriving aircraft. A flight from Washington, D.C., to Chicago, for example, is tracked by several controllers at each of four en route centers that lie between the two cities. From the last en route center, control passes to an approach controller at a Chicago airport.

As a plane comes to the boundary of a sector, the controller enters a command into the computer to hand off the flight. During the fifteen seconds that follow, the computer adds a blinking H (hand-off) to the flight's data block. At the same time, the computer displays this data block on the next controller's radar screen and causes it, along with the appended H, to blink. When this controller pushes a button to accept the hand-off, the H on the first controller's screen is replaced by an R (received) and the data block displayed on the second controller's screen stops blinking. At this point, the first controller instructs the flight crew to contact the next controller on a new radio frequency.

Taking a National View of Air Traffic

To help keep skies safe and minimize flight delays, the FAA's Air Traffic Control System Command Center computer in Washington is supplied with data about every aircraft on en route-center radar screens. Some 3,500 or more blips may appear on the display, which is updated every three minutes. The example at right shows traffic above the forty-eight states around noon on a typical August day; by touching a key, the operator can zoom in on a single sector. In this instance, the operator has instructed the system to highlight aircraft headed for six cities. The planes are represented by colored airplane symbols pointed in their direction of travel. Green planes are flying to Los Angeles, black ones to San Francisco, yellow to Denver, pink to Dallas/Fort Worth, blue to Chicago, and red to Atlanta, as indicated by the color key at the bottom of the screen. Black dots represent all other aircraft in the sky. Major airports are denoted by three-letter codes.

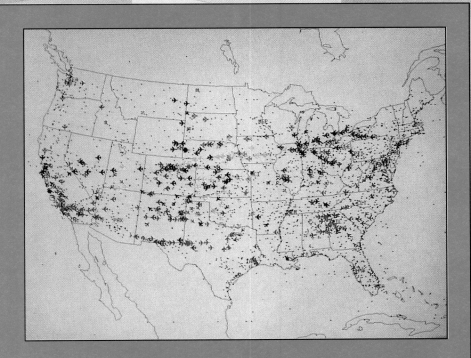

Avoiding Midair Collisions

As closely as air-traffic controllers monitor the cross-country progress of aircraft in the sky, midair collisions remain a very real peril. Near misses (the definition of a "near miss" varies depending on altitude) have more than doubled in the course of this decade. In response, flight rules have been tightened and commercial aircraft are being fitted with the Traffic Alert and Collision Avoidance System (TCAS), a computerized radar that serves as a backup for ground controllers in their efforts to keep aircraft a safe distance apart.

TCAS, which includes an advanced type of transponder that can communicate directly with a similar transponder in another plane, can alert a pilot to any aircraft, equipped with even the most rudimentary transponder, that approaches within fifteen miles.

If the intruder aircraft has an altitude-reporting transponder, the TCAS computer tracks the interloper and, based on its flight path and speed, predicts whether the two planes will approach closer to one another than allowed by flight regulations. In that event, TCAS issues a series of warnings and, if warranted, instructions for avoiding a near miss or a collision (below).

The system works whether both planes are equipped with it (overlapping spheres, opposite) or only one of them has the device installed. However, when two TCAS units are involved, they use the communications capabilities of their transponders to coordinate their instructions to the pilots so that the aircraft are not directed toward each other.

Detecting an intruder. The two spheres in the scene at left designate the surveillance areas covered by each aircraft's collision-avoidance radar. The red intruding plane has just been picked up by the blue plane's TCAS. Its computer projects that the two planes will follow the flight paths shown by the two arrows, which cross where a near miss or a collision is projected to occur unless one of the aircraft changes heading or altitude.

 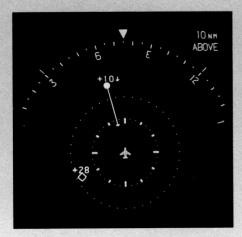 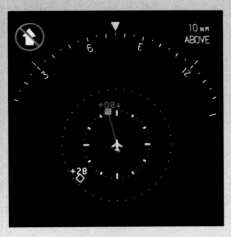

Spotting flights nearby. The TCAS monitor aboard this aircraft, indicated by the jet symbol in the center, shows two other planes (diamonds) within ten miles. The plane at lower left is flying level 2,800 feet above and five miles away. The aircraft at the top of the screen is 1,100 feet above and seven miles away, descending 500 feet per minute or faster, as indicated by the arrow. Both diamonds are white, signifying that the TCAS considers neither a threat at the moment. The scale at top is a compass.

Intruder alert. The upper aircraft now has come close enough to be a potential threat. TCAS has calculated that it will approach closer than 1,000 feet in altitude, and its symbol has changed to a solid yellow circle. The yellow "trend vector" traces the intruder's predicted path, ending where the plane is projected to be twenty-five seconds later. The system sounds an audible TRAFFIC, TRAFFIC warning to attract the pilot's attention but does not suggest evasive action at this time.

Danger at hand. Now the intruder is only 800 feet above and three miles distant, still descending. TCAS has calculated that a conflict—collision or near miss—will occur within another twenty to thirty seconds. It is time for evasive action. The yellow circle has turned into a red square, a DO NOT CLIMB symbol has appeared in the upper left corner; a synthesized voice in the cockpit confirms the warning. After the danger has passed, the blip representing the intruder disappears from the TCAS screen.

Skirting
Foul Weather

All airliners are equipped with computerized weather radar that permits a pilot to peer miles into the distance, even through clouds, to avoid thunderstorms along the route. These intense weather disturbances could pose a serious danger to aircraft—not because of the pelting rain or even vision-obscuring clouds, but because of turbulence and hail, which in diameters of half an inch or larger can break windows and decrease lift by denting a plane's wings. Hail can even dislodge the cover that protects an aircraft's radar and damage the antenna.

Looking down into the weather. Three storm cells show up fifteen to twenty-five miles ahead in this overhead, radar view of the weather. The weather system in the center is the most menacing, with a large patch of level-three precipitation *(red in the color key)*—rainfall of one-half inch to two inches per hour. A "finger" of rain to the right suggests turbulence and the possibility of hail. WX, pilot's shorthand for weather, means that the screen, which may be shared by TCAS *(pages 116-117)* and other aircraft systems, is displaying weather data. Should the plane's collision-avoidance system detect an intruder, TCAS would take control of the display until the danger of a near miss had passed.

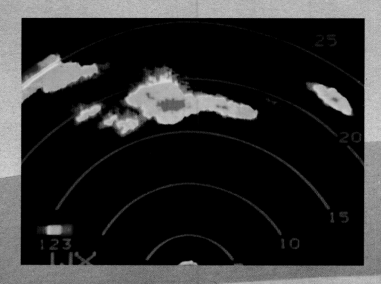

Slicing a storm. The weather radar aboard a plane surveys a thin, semicircular wedge-shaped slice of the sky ahead. The view of the slice presented on the screen is from above, not the side view the pilot would see. The slice's thickness increases with distance from the plane, and the slice can be tilted up and down to survey various levels of the sky, or even features of the terrain below.

Not every thunderstorm is accompanied by these hazards. Yet a pilot has no choice but to avoid all thunderstorms because neither turbulence nor hail can be detected directly by radar. Air movements and ice crystals, unless they are wet, do not reflect the electromagnetic waves of a radar beam to create the echoes that show up on a radar screen. Only water droplets and hail with a film of rain water do, and the difference between the two is indistinguishable on radar.

Though hampered by these limitations, weather radar, thanks to the computer, indicates in color *(left, below)* the rate of precipitation, which it can measure from the strength of the echo. Heavy precipitation, which sends a strong echo, suggests turbulence and hail. More certain signs of turbulence are frequent changes in the rate of rainfall, the colors of the display shifting rapidly from one to another. Because turbulence and hail are common where there is no rain—either above the water droplets that the radar can reveal or even below them—pilots play it safe by requesting permission from ground controllers to fly around thunderstorms, rather than over or under them.

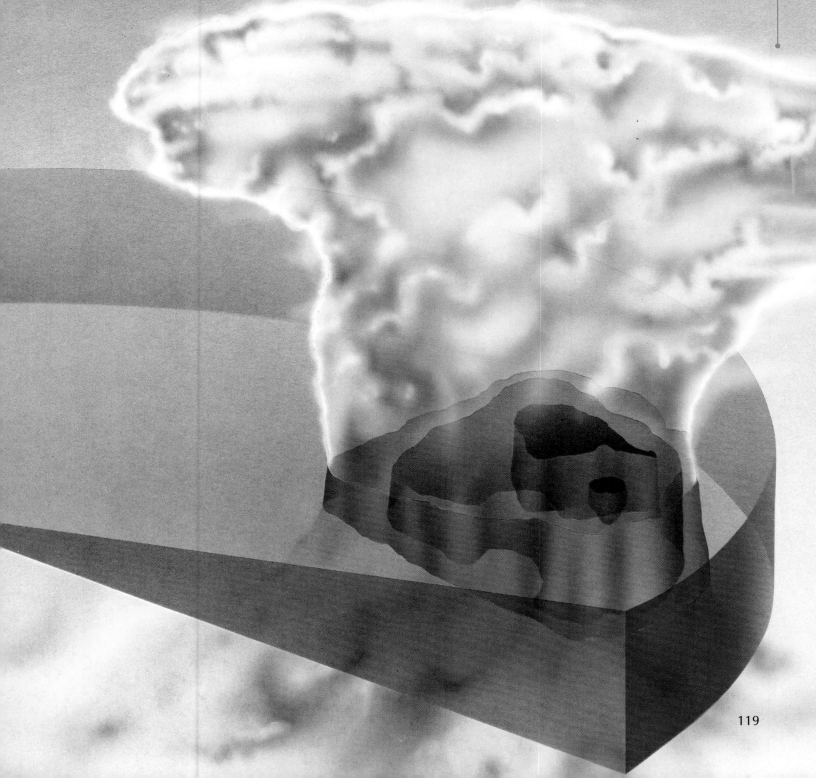

The Invisible Threat of Wind Shear

After traversing busy air corridors and dodging storms, a plane comes to the most uncertain part of the flight—landing. As the pilot approaches the runway, low altitude and speed reduce his margin for error and increase the aircraft's vulnerability to a type of turbulence known as wind shear, in which the wind suddenly changes speed or direction. At the very least, wind shear will cause a plane to bounce as it lands. At worst, it can slam an aircraft to the ground. Its most violent form, the microburst, is surprisingly common. Fifty were once detected near Chicago's O'Hare Airport in a span of forty-two days.

A deadly downdraft. A microburst, the most severe wind-shear hazard, is a powerful, concentrated downdraft that occurs in about five percent of all thunderstorms. As the air descends, the ground deflects it outward. The danger arises because air moves in one direction on one side of the microburst but in the opposite direction on the other side. When a plane flies into the microburst *(far left)*, it first meets a strong head wind, giving extra lift. In response, the pilot may even ease off on the throttle to help the craft settle toward the runway. But then the plane passes through the center of the downdraft and into a tail wind. Suddenly, the aircraft is traveling much slower relative to the air around it, reducing lift and causing the plane to fall precipitously.

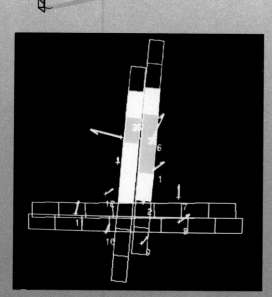

Warnings on a screen. The LLWAS computer at Denver's Stapleton Airport displays its windshear warning, calculated from measurements taken in sixty-nine triangles, as colored blocks covering parallel north-south runways. White blocks mark areas of ordinary wind shear; yellow ones signify the more hazardous microbursts. The number 35 denotes the estimated loss in airspeed encountered by a plane entering the yellow area. Arrowheads point out wind direction; arrow length indicates wind speed.

Though visible to special—and extraordinarily costly—radar designed to detect motion in anything from vehicles to air masses, wind shear is transparent to weather radar *(preceding pages)*. So at airports where wind shear poses a threat, the phenomenon is identified by comparing measurements of wind speed and direction at several points near a runway. In the advanced system illustrated here, measurements are taken by means of a computerized array of anemometers called the Low Level Windshear Alert System (LLWAS). An anemometer, drawn here to resemble a wingless model airplane, is an instrument that combines features of a weather vane and a speedometer activated by a propeller spinning in the wind.

Several times a minute, the computer samples the wind speed and direction at each anemometer. The computer averages this data and compares the result to the reading from each sensor. A substantial difference from the average in either reading suggests the presence of wind shear and causes the computer to alert the approach controller, who warns the pilot. A prudent aviator would call off the landing and try again a few minutes later, or divert to another airport.

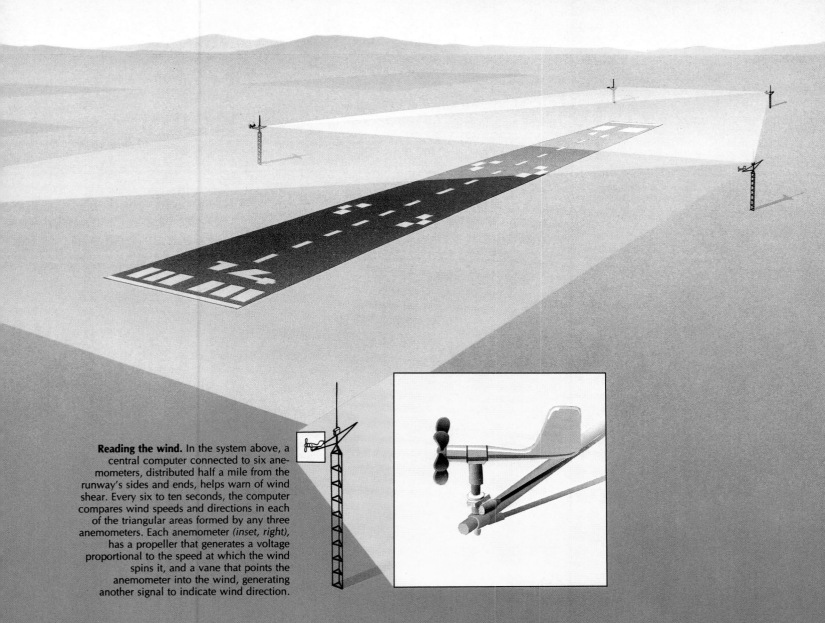

Reading the wind. In the system above, a central computer connected to six anemometers, distributed half a mile from the runway's sides and ends, helps warn of wind shear. Every six to ten seconds, the computer compares wind speeds and directions in each of the triangular areas formed by any three anemometers. Each anemometer *(inset, right),* has a propeller that generates a voltage proportional to the speed at which the wind spins it, and a vane that points the anemometer into the wind, generating another signal to indicate wind direction.

Bibliography

Books

Aircraft Owners and Pilots Association, *AOPA's Handbook for Pilots*. Frederick, Md.: Aircraft Owners and Pilots Association, 1986.

An Introduction to Inertial Navigation. Moorpark, Calif.: Litton Aero Products, 1977.

Armstrong, John H., *The Railroad—What It Is, What It Does: The Introduction to Railroading*. Omaha, Nebraska: Simmons-Boardman Publishing Corporation, 1978.

Connes, Keith, *The Loran, RNAV & NAV/COMM Guide*. Butterfield Press, 1986.

Considine, Douglas M., ed., *Van Nostrand's Scientific Encyclopedia*. New York: Van Nostrand Reinhold Company, 1983.

Deiter, Ronald H., *The Story of Metro*. Glendale, Calif.: Interurban Press, 1985.

Editors of Time-Life Books, *Space* (Understanding Computers Series). Alexandria, Va.: Time-Life Books, 1987.

Federal Aviation Administration, *National Airspace System Plan*. Washington, D.C.: U.S. Government Printing Office, June 1986.

Fujita, T. Theodore, *The Downburst*. University of Chicago: Satellite and Mesoeteorology Research Project, 1985.

Givens, Bill, *Flying with Loran C*. Blue Ridge Summit, Pa.: Tab Books Inc., 1985.

Good, John F., *The Aviators Guide to LORAN-C*. Wakefield, Mass.: Arsunai Press, 1984.

Grover, J. H. H., *Radio Aids to Air Navigation*. London: Heywood & Company Ltd., 1956.

Hewson, J. B., *A History of the Practice of Navigation*. Glasgow: Brown, Son & Ferguson, Ltd., 1983.

Homburger, Wolfgang S., *Transportation and Traffic Engineering Handbook*. Englewood Cliffs. N.J.: Prentice-Hall, Inc., 1982.

Improving Productivity in U.S. Marine Container Terminals. Washington, D.C.: National Academy Press, 1986.

King, Dick H., *Computerized Engine Control*. Albany, N.Y.: Delmar Publishers, Inc., 1987.

Knowles, Don, *The Automotive Computer*. Englewood Cliffs, N.J.: Prentice-Hall, Inc., 1987.

Koburger, Charles W., Jr., *Vessel Traffic Systems*. Centerville, Md.: Cornell Maritime Press, 1986.

Maloney, Elbert S., *Dutton's Navigation & Piloting*. Annapolis, Md.: Naval Institute Press, 1983.

May, W. E., *A History of Marine Navigation*. New York: W. Norton & Company, Inc., 1973.

Mosher, Lynn, *Automechanic's Guide to Electronic Instrumentation and Microprocessors*. Englewood Cliffs, N.J.: Prentice-Hall, Inc., 1987.

Orman, Leonard M., *Electronic Navigation*. Annapolis, Md., and North Hollywood, Calif.: Pan American Navigation Service and Weems System of Navigation, 1950.

Pozesky, Martin T., *The Air Traveler's Handbook*. New York: Simon & Schuster, 1978.

White, Harvey E., "Electricity and Magnetism," *Modern College Physics*. Princeton, N.J.: D. Van Nostrand Company, Inc., 1964.

Wilson, Mitchell, and the Editors of Time-Life Books, *Energy* (Life Science Library). New York: Time Inc., 1968.

Periodicals

Anderson, E. W., "Inertia Navigation Systems." *The Institute of Navigation; The Journal*, July 1958.

Ashjee, Javad, "Global Positioning System: Refined Processing for Better Accuracy." *Sea Technology*, March 1986.

Auld, Jack, "Ships without Sailors." *New Scientist*, Oct. 11, 1984.

Avizienis, Algirdas, "On the Achievement of a Highly Dependable and Fault-Tolerant Air Traffic Control System." *Computer*, Feb. 1987.

Basta, Nicholas, "Electronics Add Sizzle to Auto Market." *High Technology*, June 1986.

Brody, Herb, "Smart Power." *High Technology*, Dec. 1985.

Buckwalter, Lee, "Crash Recorders: New Standards, New Equipment." *Avionics*, Jan. 1983.

Collins, Richard L., "Avoidance Tactics." *Flying*, June 1987.

Cook, William, "Cars of the 90s." *U.S. News and World Report*, Aug. 10, 1987.

Dahl, Jonathan, "Danger Aloft: Evidence Suggests Many Near Misses Go Unreported." *Wall Street Journal*, July 21, 1987.

Dawkins, Oliver, "Night Passage to Normandy." *The Decca Navigator Company*, 1969.

Dawson, J. A. L., and Fred N. Brown, "Electronic Road Pricing in Hong Kong." *Traffic Engineering & Control*, Nov. 1985.

Donoghue, J. A.:
"Airbus A320 Cockpit: An Electric Experience." *Air Transport World*, April 1986.
"Airbus A320 Flight Control System." *Air Transport World*, April 1986.
"U.S. ATC System Is Threatened by Budget Cuts." *Air Transport World*, April 1986.

"EDI: Up Front with the Railroads." *Defense Transportation Journal*, June 1986.

Elmer-DeWitt, Phillip, "Driving by the Glow of a Screen." *Time*, April 20, 1987.

"Evolution of the Autopilot." *AOPA Pilot*, July 1987.

"FAA Funding Detection Technology Research." *Aviation Week & Space Technology*, Sept. 22, 1986.

Fischetti, Mark A., "Our Burdened Skies." *IEEE Spectrum*, Nov. 1986.

Fuller, Don, "Transforming the Family Car: Little Engines That Can." *High Technology*, June 1986.

Gallagher, Robert T., "Charting the Future." *Ocean Voice*, Jan. 1987.

Gray, Robert Reed, "Aviation Safety: Fact or Fiction." *Technology Review*, Aug./Sept. 1987.

Heppenheimer, T. A., "New Commercial Aircraft Promise Efficiency." *High Technology*, Feb. 1987.

Holusha, John, "The Computerization of Cars." *The New York Times*, May 15, 1984.

Hugon, P., "The Use of Computers in Merchant Ships." *The Institute of Navigation: The Journal*, April 1966.

Hunt, G. H., "Future Trends in Flight Control Systems." *The Journal of Navigation*, July 1975.

Hunt, Valerio R., and Andres Zellweger, "Strategies for Future Air Traffic Control Systems." *Computer*, Feb. 1987.

Julian, Ken, "Preventing Midair Collisions." *High Technology*, July 1985.

Kalra, Paul S., "A Green Light For Advanced Train Controls." *IEEE Spectrum,* Feb. 1979.

Kershner, R. B., "The Transit System." *The Institute of Navigation: The Journal,* April 1962.

Kinnucan, Paul, "Superfighters." *High Technology,* April 1984.

Klass, Phillip J., "FAA Nears Decision on Computer Supplier for En Route Centers." *Aviation Week & Space Technology,* July 22, 1985.

Koepp, Stephen, "High Anxiety and Rage." *Time,* July 20, 1987.

Leondes, Cornelius T., "Inertial Navigation for Aircraft." *Scientific American,* March 1970.

McClellan, J. Mac:
"The Grand Delusion." *Flying,* June 1987.
"TCAS." *Flying,* June 1987.

McCosh, Dan, and Tom Wilkinson, "Honda vs. Mazda: 4-Wheel-Steering Showdown." *Popular Science,* Aug. 1987.

McCosh, Dan, "Smart Circuits Revolutionize Auto Wiring." *Popular Science,* June 1987.

McDermott, Joseph M., "Freeway Surveillance and Control in Chicago Area." *Transportation Engineering Journal,* May 1980.

"Maiden Voyage of Wind Star a Resounding Success." *SAILA: Sail Assistance News,* Dec. 1986.

Magnuson, Ed, "Be Careful Out There." *Time,* January 12, 1987.

Malone, Frank, "Computers Revamp CP Yards." *Railway Age,* Oct. 1983.

Miliken, R. J., "Principles of Operation of NAVSTAR and System Characteristics." Global Positioning System Special Issue, *Navigation,* Journal of the Institute of Navigation, Summer 1978.

Monastersky, Richard, "Mastering the Microburst." *Science News,* March 21, 1987.

Moore, Bill, "The Secrets of the Black Boxes." *Discover,* Aug. 1986.

Newton, R. R., "The Transit System." *The Institute of Navigation: The Journal,* April 1962.

Nordwall, Bruce D., "Boeing Evaluating New Control Laws in 7J7 Advanced-Technology Simulator." *Aviation Week & Space Technology,* June 29, 1987.

Parker, Laura, "Another Delay in the Life of the World's Busiest Airport." *The Washington Post,* July 19, 1987.

Pearson, David, and John Keppel, "New Pieces in the Puzzle of Flight 007." *The Nation,* Aug. 17/24, 1985.

Perry, Tekla S., "Our Burdened Skies." *IEEE Spectrum,* Nov. 1986.

"Port Traffic System Will Integrate All Operations." *Motor Ship.* Aug. 1986.

Powell, Claud, "Early History of the Decca Navigator." *Journal of the Institute of Electronic and Radio Engineers,* June 1985.

Preble, Cecilia, "FAA to Impose Stricter Controls on TCA Operations." *Aviation Week and Space Technology,* Nov. 3, 1986.

Progressive Railroading, April 1987.

Richmond, Jeff, "Taking the Wind Out of Wind Shear." *High Technology,* May 1986.

Rogoff, Mortimer, "Electronic Charting." *Yachting,* Dec. 1985.

Rosenbauer, E. Jack, "Developments and Trends in Flight Recorders." *World Space Profile,* 1986.

"Scientists Developing Shear Warning Software" *Aviation Week & Space Technology,* Sept. 22, 1986.

Shuldiner, Herbert, "Super Smart Cars." *Popular Science,* Aug. 1984.

Sines, Guerdon S., "The Computer: A New World for Railroads." *Progressive Railroading,* Dec. 1986.

Stansell, Thomas A., Jr., "Civil GPS from a Future Perspective." *Proceedings of the IEEE,* Oct. 1983.

Stringer, F. S., "The Development of Flight Deck Displays." *The Journal of Navigation,* May 1984.

"The FAA's Advanced Automation Program." Special Issue, *Computer,* Feb. 1987.

"The Firsts For SkyTrain." *Progressive Railroading,* Dec. 1986.

"The Vital Link Between Railroads and Shippers." *Intermodal Age,* March/April 1987.

Wandzilak, Nadine, "Nationwide Rail Network Chugs Along." *Network World,* Nov. 17, 1986.

Wiener, Leonard, "All the Sights, Sounds, and Comforts of Home." *U.S. News and World Report,* Aug. 10, 1987.

Wrigley, Walter, "The History of Inertial Navigation." *The Journal of Navigation,* Jan. 1950.

Zoller, C. J., "Principles of Operation of NAVSTAR and System Characteristics." Global Positioning System Special Issue, *Navigation,* Journal of the Institute of Navigation, Summer 1978.

Zorpette, Glenn, "The Menacing Microburst." *IEEE Spectrum,* Nov. 1986.

Zygmont, Jeffrey:
"Keeping Tabs on Cars and Trucks." *High Technology,* Sept. 1986.
"Transforming the Family Car: The Chassis Gets Classy." *High Technology,* June 1986.

Other Publications

Adams, D. E., "Introduction to Inertial Navigation." *The Journal.* The Institute of Navigation, July 1956.

Aircraft Accident Report: China Airlines Boeing 747-SP, N4522V, 300 Nautical Miles Northwest of San Francisco, California, Feb. 19, 1985. Washington, D.C.: National Transportation Safety Board, March 29, 1986.

"The Application of Digital Avionic Systems in Aircraft." Joint RAeS/IEE Committee Symposium, Dec. 12, 1974.

A320 Flight Deck and Systems Briefing for Pilots. France: Airbus Industrie, 1987.

Automated Commercial System. Washington, D.C.: Department of the Treasury, U.S. Customs Service.

Automotive Electronics in the Year 2000. Prepared for International Congress on Transportation Electronics, Convergence '86, Oct. 20-22, 1986. Published by Ford Motor Company, Dearborn, Michigan.

Aviation's Indispensable Partner Turns 50. U.S. Department of Transportation.

Bosch, Robert:
Bosch Antiskid System for Passenger Cars. Division K1, Antiskid System Sales. Stuttgart, Federal Republic of Germany, 1983.

Bosch Engine Electronics. Automotive Equipment Division, Department for Technical Information. Stuttgart, Federal Republic of Germany, 1983.

Boykin, Valerie P., "Orientation Guide for Minimum TCAS II." McLean, Va.: The MITRE Corporation, 1985.

Constans, Jacques A., "Alcyone, Daughter of the Wind: The Ship of the Future." New York: The Cousteau Society, Nov. 1985.

Control System Definition Document for Potomac Yard. Alexandria, Va.: General Railway Signal Pamphlet, March 1985.

Deputy For Space Navigation Systems, Navstar Global Positioning System Joint Program Office, *GPS Navstar User's Overview.* Annapolis, Md., Arinc Research Corporation, 1986.

Engineering Features: Saab 9000. Saab-Scania AB/Saab Car Division. Nyköping, Sweden, 1986.

Federal Aviation Administration, "Central Flow Control Facility." Washington, D.C.: U.S. Department of Transportation.

Federal Aviation Administration, "Air Traffic Control." Washington, D.C.: U.S. Government Printing Office, 1984.

Federal Aviation Administration, *Airman's Information Manual— Official Guide to Basic Flight Information and ATC Procedures.* Washington, D.C.: U.S. Government Printing Office, April 9, 1987.

First 50 Years: A History of the Collins Radio Company and the Collins Divisions of Rockwell International. Cedar Rapids, Iowa: Avionics Group, Rockwell International, 1983.

"High Technology Rides the Rails." Washington, D.C.: Association of American Railroads, Office of Information and Public Affairs.

Hurley, M. J., J. L. Kramer, and D. D. Thornburg:
The GPS Control Segment and Its Service. San Diego: The Institute of Electrical and Electronics Engineers, Inc., 1976.
IEEE 1976 Position Location and Navigation Symposium (PLANS). San Diego: The Institute of Electrical and Electronics Engineers, Inc., 1976.

Meetze, Henry W. (President, Railinc Corporation) "The Railroad Industry and Data Processing," talk delivered at meeting of Data Processing Management Association, March 17, 1982.

Office of Automated Commercial Systems Operations:

ACS: Manager's Overview. Washington, D.C.: Department of the Treasury, U.S. Customs Service, Nov. 1986.
ACS Overview. Washington, D.C.: Department of the Treasury, U. S. Customs Service, 1987.

"Pechiney: A Profile," *Background Factsheet.* New York: The Cousteau Society, June 1985.

Railinc Corporation Annual Report, 1985.

"Revolutions in Research Will Benefit Railroads and Shippers." Washington, D.C.: Association of American Railroads, Office of Information and Public Affairs.

Sailing Tanker "Shin Aitoku Maru." Japan Marine Machinery Development Association, Sept. 1983.

735i. Bavarian Motor Works Auto Group. Munich, West Germany, 1987.

Sperry, *ColoRadar^{tm} Primus®— 90, Pilot's Handbook.* Phoenix, Ariz.: Sperry Corporation.

Sperry Traffic Alert and Collision Avoidance System TCAS. Honeywell.

Thompson, Steven D., *An Introduction to GPS, Everyman's Guide to Satellite Navigation.* Annapolis, Md.: Arinc Research Corporation, 1985.

Toyota Automotive Electronics. Toyota Motor Corporation, Public Affairs Department. Aichi, Japan.

Traffic Alert and Collision Avoidance System (TCAS). Annapolis, Md.: Arinc Research Corporation.

"UMLER Knows All About Freight Cars." *Tie Line* (Association of American Railroads employee newsletter), Feb. 1978.

United States Customs Service, *Importing into the United States.* Washington, D.C.: U.S. Government Printing Office, June 1986.

VAL System In Lille: Running Ahead of Expectation. Paris, France: Matra Transport.

"Wind Pioneers—Past, Present and Future." *Background Factsheet,* June 1985.

"Windstar Sail Cruises Limited." Promotional Release Material, Hill and Knowlton, Inc., New York, Spring 1987.

Wright, C. David. "Automotive Applications of Electronics." (Paper prepared for 1986 Institute of Electrical and Electronic Engineers workshop on Automotive Applications of Electronics), 1986.

Acknowledgments

The index for this book was prepared by Mel Ingber. The editors also wish to thank the following individuals and institutions for their help in the preparation of this volume: **In Japan:** Tokuyama—Aitoku Maru Co.; Tokyo—Ishikawajima-Harima, Heavy Industries Co., Ltd. **In France:** Annecy—Denis Chaillot, Scetauroute Annecy; Bagnac Cedex—David Villupilai, Airbus Industrie; Bron—Bernard Buttion and Michel Perard, C.E.T.E.; Le Havre—Francois Faurey, Société Nouvelle des Ateliers et Chantiers du Havre; Paris—Bertrand Charrier, Ingénieur; Maryse Ohanessian, Service Publicité Aerospatiale; Vanves—Philippe Louste, Matra Transports. **In Switzerland:** Bellinzona—Ingegnere Glauco Nolli, Bellinzona. **In the United States:** Arizona—Phoenix: Robert W. Haak, Sperry Commercial Flight Systems Division, Honeywell Inc.; California—Irvine: Vahe Z. Kludjan, Mazda, Inc.; West Los Angeles: George Casper and Frank Sutschek, Teledyne Controls; Colorado—Boulder: Wayne Sand and Wes Wilson, National Center for Atmospheric Research; District of Columbia—William B. Harper, Washington National Tower; Mortimer Rogoff, Digital Directions Company, Inc.; Thomas J. Falvey, Adeste Fuentes, and Michael Sakahara, U.S. Coast Guard; Joseph J. Fee, Tim Grovac, Sam Rosenzweig, Richard Stafford, and Thomas Williamson, Federal Aviation Administration; Henry M. Meetze and Janet Smith, RAILINC Corporation; Florida—Sarasota: Barry Hawkins and Dave Schmidtman, Fairchild Weston Systems Inc.; Maryland—Annapolis: John D. Hill, Peter A. Scala, U.S. Naval Academy; Michigan—Farmington Hills: Josef Mack, Robert Bosch Corporation; Warren: Anthony V. Galliardi, Ollie T. McCarter, and William E. Vergin, General Motors; Missouri—St. Louis: Tim Hogan, Union Pacific Railroad; Nebraska—Omaha: John Bromley, Union Pacific Railroad; New Jersey—Hasbrouck Heights: Pietro Ghisleni, Fiat Auto U.S.A., Inc.; Virginia—Charlottesville: Thomas Braithwaite, Sperry Marine; Leesburg: Wayne C. Bevan, Paul Bringer, Naomi Karkanen, and Charles R. Reavis, Washington ARTCC; Norfolk: Kathryn Hill, SAILA; Washington—Renton: Elizabeth Reese and Marve Wehrman, Boeing Commercial Airplane Co.

Picture Credits

Index

Time-Life Books is a division of Time Life Inc., a wholly owned subsidiary of
THE TIME INC. BOOK COMPANY

TIME-LIFE BOOKS

MANAGING EDITOR: Thomas H. Flaherty
Director of Editorial Resources:
Elise D. Ritter-Clough
Director of Photography and Research:
John Conrad Weiser
Editorial Board: Dale M. Brown, Roberta Conlan, Laura Foreman, Lee Hassig, Jim Hicks, Blaine Marshall, Rita Thievon Mullin, Henry Woodhead

PUBLISHER: Joseph J. Ward

Associate Publisher: Trevor Lunn
Editorial Director: Donia Ann Steele
Marketing Director: Regina Hall
Director of Design: Louis Klein
Production Manager: Marlene Zack
Supervisor of Quality Control: James King

Editorial Operations
Production: Celia Beattie
Library: Louise D. Forstall
Computer Composition: Deborah G. Tait (Manager), Monika D. Thayer, Janet Barnes Syring, Lillian Daniels

Correspondents: Vanessa Kramer (London); Maria Vincenza Aloisi (Paris); Ann Natanson (Rome); Dick Berry (Tokyo). Valuable assistance was also provided by: Wibo van de Linde (Amsterdam); Elizabeth Brown and Christina Lieberman (New York).

UNDERSTANDING COMPUTERS

SERIES DIRECTOR: Lee Hassig
Series Administrator: Loretta Britten

Editorial Staff for *Transportation*
Designer: Robert K. Herndon
Associate Editors: Jean Crawford (pictures), Peter Pocock (principal), Roberta Conlan, Allan Fallow, Thomas H. Flaherty
Researchers: Stephanie A. Lewis, Gwen C. Mullen
Writer: Robert M. S. Somerville
Assistant Designer: Susan Deal-Daniels
Copy Coordinator: Elizabeth Graham
Picture Coordinator: Renée DeSandies
Editorial Assistant: Susan L. Finken

Special Contributors: Joseph Alper, Mark A. Bello, Sarah Burke, David Darling, Richard A. Jenkins, Martin Mann, Marilynne Rudnick, Charles Smith, Brooke Stoddard, John R. Sullivan (text); Julia Anderson, Richard A. Davis, Tracey Funn, Julie Ann Trudeau, Hattie A. Wicks (research).

CONSULTANTS

ROBERT L. BARLEY is assistant vice-president of information and communications systems with the Union Pacific Railroad in St. Louis, Missouri. He played a leading role in developing Union Pacific's computer systems.

W. J. CARLSON has been supervisor of signals and communications at the Potomac Yard of the Richmond, Fredericksburg & Potomac Railroad in Alexandria, Virginia, since 1973. He is responsible for operating and maintaining the yard's computerized communications and control equipment.

MARTIN LUKES is a senior engineer at the Washington Metropolitan Area Transit Authority in Washington, D.C., where he oversees the design and testing of automatic train-control systems.

DENNIS GROSSI, an investigator at the National Transportation Safety Board in Washington, D.C., uses computer graphics and information from flight-data recorders to analyze airplane accidents.

RICHARD A. PEAL has over thirty years experience in avionics, and as the chief engineer for Flight Management Systems of Boeing Commercial Airplane Company in Seattle, Washington, he designs and tests integrated flight systems that connect major control-, sensor-, and instrument-related functions of an aircraft.

D. RAY STURGES is manager of transportation services at the Potomac Yard of the Richmond, Fredericksburg & Potomac Railroad in Alexandria, Virginia, where he oversees computerized communication among the railroad's clients.

RUSSELL TAYLOR is an automotive instructor specializing in electronics and fuel systems at Northern Virginia Community College in Alexandria, Virginia. He has also worked as an automobile technician and is certified by the National Institute for Automotive Service Excellence.

C. DAVID WRIGHT is project manager for the Computer Systems Development Group of General Motors Corporation in Warren, Michigan. A graduate of the General Motors Institute, he also holds a master's degree in electrical engineering from Stanford University.

REVISIONS STAFF

EDITOR: Lee Hassig

Writer: Esther Ferington
Assistant Designer: Bill McKenney
Copy Coordinator: Donna Carey
Picture Coordinator: Leanne G. Miller

Consultant: Paul Ceruzzi, a historian of computer science, is curator in the Department of Space History at the National Air and Space Museum.

Library of Congress Cataloging in Publication Data

Transportation / by the editors of Time-Life Books. — Rev. ed.
p. cm. — (Understanding computers)
Includes bibliographical references and index.
ISBN 0-8094-7606-1
1. Transportation engineering—Data processing.
2. Transportation—Automation. 3. Automobiles—Electronic equipment. I. Time-Life Books. II. Series.
TA1145.T69 1991
629.04'0285—dc20   91-14679
                                                         CIP

For information on and a full description of any of the Time-Life Books series listed, please write:
Reader Information
Time-Life Customer Service
P.O. Box C-32068
Richmond, Virginia 23261-2068